C000213626

Also by Lisa Ch

Conversations that Make a Difference for Children and Young People:
Relationship-Focused Practice from the Frontline

In this unique book, international trainer and consultant Lisa Cherry
invites professionals from education, social work and healthcare to
engage in conversations on a range of pertinent topics and issues
affecting children and young people today.

Divided into three main parts, which introduce attachment, adversity and trauma, each discussion places an emphasis on emotion and
the understanding that we have as humans for compassion, empathy
and connection. By encouraging collaboration between sectors and
exploring a range of intersecting themes, the conversations take the
reader on a winding journey to broaden their depth of thinking, reflect
on their practice and to consider the central message: that we can
bring about social change, one interaction at a time.

This book is a call to action and an opportunity to look around and decide what kind of service we want to provide, what kind of community we want to live in and what sort of legacy we want to leave. At a time of ever-present social and political challenges, this book will stimulate conversations on current practice and professional development for the future and is a must-read for everyone working with children and young people.

Lisa Cherry is not only a great thinker and writer, she's a deeply wise, insightful, courageous, loving and humane presence, with a truly remarkable capacity to communicate how she transformed her childhood of neglect, pain and trauma, including being in care from the age of 13, into a life of personal growth, healing and helping the vulnerable. The other immensely impressive care experienced adults she brings together to tell their stories in this wonderful book do the same. The result is a truly inspirational book that provides the vital ingredient of hope that is usually missing from such analyses, along with countless insights into how vulnerable children, adults and families can be helped.

Professor Harry Ferguson, Department of Social Work and Social Care, University of Birmingham

This new edition of *The Brightness of Stars* powerfully captures the lives of adults who have experienced care. It is an enlightening book which includes their current reflections on their original stories told in 2013, as well as additional contributions. There is much to learn in these stories about how care casts a long shadow on their adult lives, as well the development of resilience in adulthood through love, education, human agency, support and self-fulfilment.

This book is essential reading for all those who work with care experienced young people and adults, as well as those who care about how society does or does not care for its most vulnerable children.

Professor Mike Stein, University of York, author of 'Care Less Lives: The Story of the Rights Movement of Young People in Care'

Profound and deeply moving, these personal accounts of care experienced individuals speak of their courage, strength and resilience in the face of adversity. Skilfully and sensitively curated by Lisa Cherry, who also shares her own story, this is a masterclass for those of us seeking to learn by walking in the shoes of those with lived experience. Please do read this book. It has given me new insight into myself and into the work that has been my life's passion.

Charlotte Ramsden, Strategic Director for People, Salford City Council

The contributors to this collection (all, but one, raised in care as children) are of various ages and cross the generations. Their chapters are like a Christmas bran tub, full of gifts of different shapes and sizes. That the stories also run the gamut of care experiences, from the positive to the traumatic, reflects the kaleidoscopic reality of that experience. It is a particularly welcome feature of the book since, it challenges the tendency to stereotype both the care experience and those who go through it. For me, reading through the chapters was like sitting there as a child, on Christmas morning, surrounded by wrapping paper and delighted by the variety of presents I'd uncovered.

Dr Jim Goddard, Chair of The Care Leavers' Association

In providing this third edition of *The Brightness of Stars* Lisa Cherry gives another opportunity for over 10 adults (herself included) to reflect on how their lives, before during and after being 'in care', have shaped who they are now. It also provides the chance for some to 'update' and add further reflection. They each had a different journey through childhood and beyond, not least because entry to care came for some (welcome or as a profound shock) after time with their first families, and for others before they had known their families. Even acknowledging that there is no such thing as a 'typical' in-care experience, these are far from 'familiar' stories as these are some of the, thankfully growing number, of 'bright stars', those who in their own estimations and those whose lives they have touched are making a success of their lives. The stories told are personal, and more about their internal responses to what life in care did *to* rather than did *for* these individuals. They tell us little about the detail of being in foster or residential care. But they remind us that 'care' is a necessary public service, and provide messages about how it can do better. Despite some upsetting statistics and shocking stories, most who need to come into care do 'well enough', and most do better than if they had remained at home without the services their families would have needed. But, as Lisa Cherry reminds us, children who need to come into care are – each in their own way – special. They all need love and parenting, but 'Good Enough' parenting for these children is not good enough – they all need the Very Best Parenting, 'Parenting Extraordinaire'.

June Thoburn, Emeritus Professor of Social Work, University of East Anglia

The Brightness of Stars

In this poignant book, Lisa Cherry brings together a collection of candid and personal reflections on the care system in the UK, offering alternative ways of thinking about the care experience, supporting better ways of working, and providing justification for a trauma-informed lens to be applied to all forms of work with those in care.

Through personal insights and reflections, the book brings often-unheard stories vividly to life, beginning with the author's own. These are stories about love and pain; hurt and isolation; the depth of lived experience that makes up a life; how we live our lives through our relationships with others and where we feel we fit in. In this thoughtfully compiled third edition, original contributors look back on their own reflections from the lives that they live now, new stories bring new perspectives, and discussion points provide the opportunity to consider the realities of the care experience as well as life beyond.

Whilst each story is unique, shared themes reveal the truth of the care system and, coming at a time where there is a real opportunity for change, the narratives in this book are ultimately stories of hope and connection. This is crucial reading for policy makers, those working in social work, education and adoption, as well as care experienced adults.

Lisa Cherry is a leading international trainer and consultant, specialising in assisting professionals working with vulnerable children and families to understand trauma, recovery and resilience. Lisa brings nearly three decades of working in educational and social care settings and a 30-year journey of recovery in overcoming her own experiences of trauma.

The Brightness of Stars

Stories from Care Experienced Adults to Inspire Change

3rd Edition

Lisa Cherry

Routledge
Taylor & Francis Group

LONDON AND NEW YORK

Cover image: © Dani Pasteau

Third edition published 2022
by Routledge
4 Park Square, Milton Park, Abingdon, Oxon, OX14 4RN

and by Routledge
605 Third Avenue, New York, NY 10158

Routledge is an imprint of the Taylor & Francis Group, an informa business

First edition published by Wilson King Publishing, 2013

Second edition published by Kate Cairns Associates 2016

British Library Cataloguing-in-Publication Data
A catalogue record for this book is available from the British Library

Library of Congress Cataloging-in-Publication Data
A catalog record has been requested for this book

ISBN: 978-1-032-19157-7 (hbk)
ISBN: 978-1-032-19158-4 (pbk)
ISBN: 978-1-003-25796-7 (ebk)

DOI: 10.4324/9781003257967

Typeset in Optima
by Deanta Global Publishing Services, Chennai, India

Contents

Contents

Foreword

It was an honour to be asked to write the Foreword for this book. I recall seeing the first edition of *The Brightness of Stars* some years ago. It struck me that the subtitle – *Stories of Adults Who Came Through the Care System* – was, itself, a bright star in an otherwise dark sky. Looked after children, especially adults who used to be looked after, are strikingly invisible in UK social policy.

Logically, this is odd. After all, the 0.5 per cent or so of children who go through the UK care system are, quite literally, 'children of the welfare state'. Far more than any other children, they are – or should be – the focus of child welfare policy. You won't find them, though, in most mainstream social policy textbooks; or, with rare and tiny exceptions, in the memoirs of even those UK Ministers (of Health and Education) who held formal, legal responsibility for them. They are like children who have been kept in the attic.

In a modern world in which different social and ethnic groups are gaining an increasing sense of their history, separate from the mainstream histories we were all taught at school, those in the care system remain an exception. Their childhoods take place in a largely undocumented world. Books such as this, therefore, offer a rare way of accessing a shared history. It is a history that several hundred thousand adults in the UK have lived through. It is one which, particularly for pre-internet generations, was often lived in an isolated bubble of childhood trauma and, when adult, a colossal focus, by the world around us, on mainstream family life – a focus which usually shoved over the edge, never mind to the margins, other experiences of childhood.

In bringing together the stories of others from the care system, alongside her own, Lisa has performed a signal service to those of us who have grown up in care. I still recall the shock of recognition I felt, in the 1980s, on reading some of the early publications from the National Association of Young People in Care (NAYPIC) (see Sean's chapter for more on the work of NAYPIC back then). In the modern world, we are replete with information and, for example, adult care leavers are more aware that they are not alone. Nowadays, social media facilitates the sharing of life stories, and care leavers are among those who have made use of its opportunities. One might, therefore, think that a book such is this would be less necessary. However, the reverse is true. The ability to step back, to consider the ties that knit our past to our present, is central to our ability to take control of our lives. In a raging sea of information, it can be our anchor.

Moreover, the power of the written word to connect, sooth and heal is too easily forgotten in a world saturated by audio-visual media. For example, when people discuss their love of a particular book that holds meaning for their lives, their enthusiasm generally drowns the more tepid affection they feel for certain films, music and other media. This is because books – as all religions know – have the power to touch the soul in ways that other media cannot. Somewhere out there, now, are people whose souls will be touched by one or more of the accounts in this collection.

There is another gain from this book. Because of the different ages of its contributors, it gives us snapshots of British social history, and of the history of the care system, that stretch back generations. We are reminded of ways in which the world has changed and of ways in which it hasn't. Anyone with an interest in British social history will gain from that.

As Lisa points out in her introduction, sharing one's story of growing up in care can be a somewhat risky business. From those who haven't experienced growing up in care – i.e. the vast majority of adults – there can come, often mixed together, incomprehension, pity and scepticism. Despite our ever-expanding media world, we mostly remain surrounded by people with no comprehension of the care system. This can include our partners in life and our closest friends. In such a context, it takes sensitivity to take the life stories of adult care leavers and weave them into a book. Lisa Cherry was clearly the right person to do so. Her work in other areas, added to her own care background, gives her the skills to handle the precious collection of reflections and memories that she delivers to us. She handles them with the singular focus of someone carrying a crystal vase across a polished wooden floor.

The snapshot memories that the book is peppered with are a reminder that our adult lives – for all of us, not just those in care – are often interrupted by vivid memories from our childhood. Sometimes important things are recalled and trivia forgotten. Sometimes it is the other way around. The forgotten experiences may be swimming about in our subconscious, but the things we remember are filtered through our adult understanding and add to our sense of who we are as adults. We may replay them repeatedly and, over the decades, come to interpret them differently with the wisdom of age.

However, while much of our wisdom and growth, as adults, comes from reflection on our past, we can also learn from the experiences of others. The reflections in this collection are likely to resonate with many others who grew up in care. How many of us have looked at an early experience positively and then, a decade later, negatively, or vice versa, as some of these authors have done? Age brings more aches and pains, for sure; but it also brings perspective.

In adding fresh stories from adult care leavers, and fresh opportunities to reflect on the original stories, Lisa has provided both greater depth and range to the book. This widens its reach. The discussion points offer reflections available to any reader, but perhaps especially to students and professionals who work, have worked or will work with looked after children. We see, in this collection, a variety of parents, siblings, social workers, residential workers and foster carers, all interacting with the subjects of the book. They come and go, weaving their way into the lives of children. Their involvement is often transient, but their impacts, both good and bad, can last a lifetime. We also come across the routine practices of the post-war care system – six-monthly reviews, swift moves without consultation, random exposure to abuse – but, on this occasion, from the perspective of those who were once children at the heart of these practices and decisions.

All this contributes to filling an enormous gap in our public stock of knowledge. The relationship between the adult and child selves of former looked after children is too little explored. Academic research in this area echoes the system itself; it tends to follow the money and, therefore, to focus only on looked after children up to the point at which they are no longer the concern of the State. Most parents don't do this. They worry about the kind of adults their children will become; they look ahead to grandchildren; they sometimes take in their children if their lives fall apart in their twenties, thirties, forties. The role of being a parent never ends – unless that parent is the State.

Small snippets resonated with me personally: Lisa's discussion of the politics of food, for example. Everyone will have their own points of connection. In some cases, for instance, it might be the reflections of the authors from when they, in turn, became parents. Personally, of course, I most see the value of this book to fellow care leavers. There were, certainly, multiple resonances with my own care experience, in the 1960s and 1970s. However, it is also easy to see the book's wider value. This is because it has the virtue of being very gently filtered (by the requirements of the book format). It isn't overlain with an aca-demic researcher's typical focus on structures, theoretical models and methodology. These can easily drown out the voices of the subjects of research. Moreover, the facts and legislation with which Lisa peppers her account add context to the individual accounts. They make clear the importance and scale of this area of British social history.

One point that Lisa makes particularly resonated. If this collection suggests anything it is the colossal avoidance of the pain of children that the past care system has indulged in. The child welfare system continues to focus on the one-tenth of the visible iceberg of trauma, ignoring the nine-tenths which it now, after many decades of academic research, has no excuse for not addressing. The development of a genuinely therapeutic care system is long overdue. The majority of children have always entered care due to their experience of abuse and neglect. The traumatic consequences of such experiences, and of the rupturing of relationships that typically occurs on entry into care, have, by and large, been routinely ignored for generations.

Finally, Lisa's conclusion echoes my own thoughts after reading this collection, particularly her point about the relevance of luck to her own experience. One often comes across documentaries in which old soldiers are interviewed about their war experiences. They frequently bristle at any notion that they are 'heroes'. This is because war has taught them the sheer random power of luck. They know that they survived while others died for no other reason than the direction of a bullet. On reading these experiences, one is repeatedly struck by the relevance of luck. The peculiar randomness of the care system puts a premium on luck in ways which usually don't apply in the more stable world of most families.

Every adult carries within themselves the child they once were. Each person we meet thus contains both the infant and the teenager of their past. It's a point worth remembering in our age of swift judgement amid the everyday push and shove of life. This book encourages us to do that remembering. It is therefore a gift and, like all gifts, deserves to be shared.

Dr Jim Goddard is a retired university academic. He has been the Chair of The Care Leavers' Association (www.careleavers.com) since 2011, and grew up in children's homes in Liverpool and Birkenhead in the 1960s and 1970s.

Preface

As I sit down to write in this, the third edition of *The Brightness of Stars*, I do so in the context of a number of areas that continue to impact those living in care, those coming out of care and adults who have been children in care. The contextualisation of current times feels important as the stories in this book span many decades, many policies and many different governments in power.

Firstly, there is a hugely contentious review of children's social care under way which has a timeframe so small that its results will have long been published before you are able to read this book. The review was offered to those who have waited a long time for it as an independent review, a once in a lifetime opportunity and with a "bold and broad scope" (Department for Education, 2021a). However, according to the British Association of Social Workers, it has been accused of being rushed, lacking in transparency and in denial about the impact of austerity (BASW, 2021).

Secondly, there is the thorny issue of unregulated accommodation for looked after children aged 16 and 17 years, accommodation which has included 'provisions' such as hostels and caravan parks (Blackwell, 2021). In September 2021, a ban came into force on placing children under 16 in care in unregulated accommodation. No such ban exists for children in care aged between 16 and 18 (Department for Education, 2021b). Finally, a report into sexual abuse in Lambeth Council's children's homes across many decades was also recently released. More than 705 former residents came forward with their harrowing experiences of abuse, neglect and abandonment (Sodha, 2021).

Nestled deep within the numbers, the data and the news headlines there are stories – human stories. These are the messy reality of the experience of being in care as a child. There is a discomfort in writing about oneself, about writing up these stories, when it is not to be a private endeavour; yet the reasons for doing so can be compelling. For me, personally, the writing of this book, initially in 2013, provided a phenomenal amount of healing from experiences that I had pushed to one side, struggled to articulate and carried a lot of shame from. I am also told that the stories within the book generated a sense of connection and belonging for others with the same experiences. There are many updates in this edition; the inclusion of new chapters, discussion points and reflections. It is my hope that the sense of belonging and connection can be even more reachable.

The book is divided into three parts. Part One is my story as I understood it when I first wrote it, and from the perspective, knowledge and understanding that I had at the time. That's all we ever have really; but it has been quite confronting to read through my story as it was for me then. The hurt and pain that are at the fore in all their unresolved glory are no longer unresolved. In leaving it as it is the reader is reminded that we change over time. For this reason, I have made very few changes but, instead, have added reflections at the end of each chapter with the perspective, knowledge and understanding that I have today, reflecting growth and changes across the years passed since I first sat down with my laptop.

Part Two has the same stories within it that featured in the original edition, apart from one person's. I was unable to find Caroline for her reflection, and therefore for her permission to be included in this edition. However, I have been able to contact everyone else and they have provided a reflection piece on where they are now. In addition, there are discussion points within each chapter.

Part Three offers five new chapters bringing new stories and providing an opportunity for us to think further about what makes a difference in those developmental years to life course trajectories. I have continued the theme of having a word for each chapter that resonates with each story.

The contributors in this book offer so many other narratives than the ones traditionally available. Some of the narratives that have been the most frustrating to observe and have also been directed at me over the years have been pity – "you poor thing"; saviour complex – "I can rescue you though"; hero worship – "you're amazing and oh so special to have overcome so much"; and poor outcome dwellers – "do you know how many people who've been in care end up in prison?" This book offers the reader so much more to support their thinking about and understanding of adults with care experience. It provides different ways of thinking about the experience, supports better ways of working, and is ultimately a call to action for a trauma-informed lens to be applied to all that is involved in working with children who are in care. More than this, the call to action asks that this trauma-informed lens is applied to the adults who we meet, in whatever capacity, who have this back story interwoven into their development.

References

BASW (2021) BASW England policy statement on the Independent review of children's social care. Retrieved from https://www.basw.co.uk/media/news/2021/feb/basw-england-policy-statement-independent-review-children%E2%80%99s-social-care on 7 August 2021.

Blackwell, A. (2021) DfE failure to ban unregulated provision for under-18s will leave teenagers at risk, warn sector heads. *Community Care*, 23 February. https://www.communitycare.co.uk/2021/02/23/dfe-failure-ban-unregulated-provision-18s-will-leave-teenagers-risk-warn-sector-heads/.

Department for Education (2021a) Terms of reference for the independent review of children's social care: a bold and broad approach to support a fundamental review of children's experiences. Retrieved from https://assets.publishing.service.gov.uk/government/uploads/system/uploads/attachment_data/file/952624/terms_of_reference_independent_childrens_social_care_review.pdf on 7 August 2021.

Department for Education (2021b) Unregulated accommodation banned for vulnerable children under 16. Press release, 19 February. https://www.gov.uk/government/news/unregulated-accommodation-banned-for-vulnerable-children-under-16.

Sodha, S. (2021) When moral pieties get in the way of doing the right thing, children suffer. *Guardian*, 1 August. https://www.theguardian.com/commentisfree/2021/aug/01/when-moral-pieties-get-in-the-way-of-doing-the-right-thing-children-suffer.

Acknowledgements

I would like to take this opportunity to thank everyone who contributed to this book because to do so was to dig deep, really deep – and I imagine sometimes when they didn't want to – so that they too could share their stories. The generosity of sharing personal insights and reflections of complex childhood experiences should never be underestimated. I am also deeply grateful to Chrissy Kelly for her incredible poetry that wraps the book in a hug, and to Fiona Holiday for her beautiful illustrations.

I have so much gratitude for the experiences that I had as a child and young person as they are the very experiences that put fire in my belly and put me on a professional trajectory that has meant that I can say that I have never worked a day in my life. It has never felt like work. I have tended to my heart's desires, waking up every day with a passion for creating change for children and young people and the adults that they will become.

A big thank you must go to all my wonderful supportive friends who are really my family, and also to the amazing online community that stretches globally, of which I am massively a part.

It is my children, who are now adults with their own challenges, carrying their own intergenerational histories, that I must credit with teaching me how to be a mother; teaching me how to love.

Finally, I must thank Clare and Leah from Routledge for believing in the potential of this book to make a difference and supporting a third edition.

Contributors

Carrie has spent the last ten years working directly with young care leavers to support them in the many paths of transition. Recently she has taken a path towards academia, is currently completing her master's degree in Childhood Youth and Social Policy, and is due to start a doctorate looking at the financial needs and barriers to care leavers in transition.

LinkedIn: Carrie Wilson-Harrop.

Chrissy is a poet, a successful qualified advisory teacher, and holds a BA Hons in Information Technology, a diploma in Experiential Counselling Chichester College and an HND in Computing Information Systems. Chrissy's lived experience from two foster homes and two children's homes means she is passionate about support for young people's life chances; and she believes that education, traditional and non-traditional, and even just one adult who supports you in life are keys to success. She has one grown-up son, loves to travel and remains a student of life.

You can connect with her via her online training at www.fabulousthinking.com, where she runs courses to support the understanding of how the human experience works through thought. She also loves a chat on Twitter @fab_thinking and connecting on Instagram @ chrissy_kelly.

Dianne has been happily married for nearly 40 years. She lives in Sussex with her husband, where their latest project has been renovating a 17th-century farmhouse. However, for over three years she has also been supporting members of her family through challenging health issues. Nutrition remains an important part of her life, and Dianne continues to explore this fascinating area. Her focus in recent years has been healthy ageing, and she hopes to return to health coaching in 2022. Keep an eye on her website for further updates (www.lifenourishment.co.uk).

Isabelle is a firm believer in all things theatre, change and improving life for all care experienced people. A graduate of the Royal Central School of Speech and Drama with a first-class honour's degree in Drama, Applied Theatre and Education, Isabelle spent time from the age of nine in the care system, and was about to 'age out' in January 2022, at the scary age of 25. Her current projects include Reclaim Care – a care experienced collective focused on healing together, supporting each other, understanding our shared histories, and imagining possible futures; and Us to You – a spoken word piece in direct response to all non-care experienced people and the things they have labelled us with.

Get in touch with Isabelle on Twitter @IsabelleKirkham; read their work on medium @isabellekirkham; support them on KO-FI (https://ko-fi.com/isabellekirkham97).

Jamie is a counsellor and psychotherapist working with adults and groups in London and Brighton. Jamie is passionate about trauma-informed, intersectional and culturally sensitive practice. As a member of the Diversity and Ability (D&A) community and the Aashna Counselling and Psychotherapy creative team, he is engaged in developing 1:1 and group work and training exploring difference, diversity and intersectionality including care experience. Jamie is the co-author/editor of *Study Skills for Students with Dyslexia: Support for Specific Learning Differences (SpLDs)* (SAGE Publications). He is one of many members of Reclaim Care, a collective of care experienced and allies focused on healing together, understanding our shared histories and imagining possible futures.

Contact details: jamiecrabbtherapy.com; aashna.uk; reclaimcare.uk; diversityandability.com.

Jane has spent many years teaching women returners to education (she taught many assertiveness skills and Women's Studies on an Access to Higher Education course at a local Further Education College). After studying for a master's in Women's Studies, she trained as a counsellor and helped victims of domestic violence and abuse in a voluntary capacity. Always an active trade unionist in all her workplaces, she then worked as a national officer in Training and Equalities at the head office of a teachers' trade union. From this she returned to education and became the first ever (in the UK) non-Muslim woman head teacher at a Muslim school for girls.

Jane's interests and passion then took her into the field of childhood trauma and attachment and working with extremely vulnerable children: firstly, as the head of a Pupil Referral Unit working with children who had been permanently excluded from mainstream school; and, finally, as the deputy head of a virtual school working solely with children in the care system across various local schools. She ensured that both her children graduated from university, and both are successful in their own fields. Even in semi-retirement, Jane continues to work with vulnerable children and is a member of the Attachment Research Community's (ARC) campaign to improve emotional well-being and inclusion of children and young people. Her work continues to change minds about care experienced children. Meanwhile, she continues on her own journey to personal fulfilment and growth, and is happier and more content than at any other time in her life. She is open to discussion and support for projects and research in the field of care experienced trauma and resilience, and is looking forward to writing her own story.

Contact details: janecollins1@gmx.com.

Pav is an equality and employment law specialist. His professional career has spanned the public, private and voluntary sectors. He has served as director of UNI Global Union in Switzerland, where he helped negotiate a UN convention preventing violence against women at work and a UN global compact on migration. A central tenet of Pav's work has been the defence of human rights. He was Head of Equality in the UK's Department of Education, a Public Appointments Ambassador in the Government Equalities Office, and an employment tribunal member in the Ministry of Justice. Pav remains active as a Director of Strategy at the award-winning UK Black Pride.

Pav is Governor of Lancashire Teaching Hospitals NHS Trust, leads the equality work at Lancashire and South Cumbria NHS Trust, and is an elected councillor on Preston City Council.

Having left his care home in Lancashire, Pav went on to gain a BA (Hons) and an MA from the University of Cambridge, as well as an MA in Labour Economics from L'Università Degli Studi di Torino in Italy.

Rosie is a Doctoral Researcher at University of Southampton under the supervision of Ms Rebecca Smith. The focus of her research is representations of orphans and care leavers in fiction, which she is examining through the lens of both creative and critical practice. The creative piece explores her experiences of leaving care as well as considering the positive aspect that reading fiction has had on her life.

She has worked on many projects and was a Research Assistant in the Department of Experimental Psychology, University of Oxford. Conversations for Care #CareConvos was a knowledge exchange project co-created with Dr Aoife O'Higgins. They held monthly Twitter chats and outreach activities at Magdalen College. Care in the time of Covid was a project that explored the day-to-day lives of care experienced adults in the UK during the pandemic.

Rosie is currently working in collaboration with Dr Dee Michell (University of Adelaide) on Care Experience & Culture, a digital archive – the first of its kind that features care experienced literature, spoken word, academic material, sport and film/TV.

Twitter: @rosie_canning.

Sean is a founding member of the National Association of Young People in Care (NAYPIC), a children's rights advocacy organisation that was run by young people in and ex care. Sean spent nearly ten years (1980–1989) developing NAYPIC, setting up local groups and heading up various campaigns that took the social services head on. Sean compiled the first ever national review of the views of young people in care in the UK, extensive research of care experienced people's views that formed the verbal evidence from NAYPIC to the 1983–84 Parliamentary Children In Care Select Committee. Sean was highly commended by Renée Short, who chaired that committee. Many of the policies that Sean compiled from the views of young people in care made their way into the Children's Act 1989.

Sean was a board member of the Children's Legal Centre and on the original steering committee setting up Black and In Care, just one of a number of major issues that came out of his report 'Sharing Care'. He directed, edited and produced NAYPIC's *Speak Out* and *Black and In Care*, the first videos ever made to convey a range of care experienced views.

Sean is a graduate of the National Film School, and has made films in children's homes, hostels and foster homes - among his extensive video and viral campaigning work for many large-scale charities. He has also worked in broadcast TV for the BBC, ITV, Ch4, TRG and HBO as a director of drama, all the while mentoring young people in care.

Sean plays a fundamental part in the newly formed Care Experienced Policy Group. He still makes videos, and also writes about the complexity around a wide range of care issues on his website (seangeoghegan.com).

Shaunna is 23 years old and a care experienced young woman who is currently a doctoral student in psychology and neuroscience at Liverpool John Moores University. Shaunna was awarded the Pro-Vice Chancellor Scholarship to undertake a three-year PhD starting in February 2021. The PhD is titled "Pathways to Social-Connectedness in Care Experienced Young People", a project which aims to investigate the social, emotional and psychological factors that predict social connectedness in care experienced people. Her research to date has explored the health and social impact of early life adversity.

Shaunna has a passion for using research to improve the wellbeing and health of care experienced people and to empower them to thrive in life. She has a profound interest in improving standards of social care and is an active member of several groups with that aim. Outside of academia she enjoys advocacy work and regularly helps raise awareness of the care system by helping to dismantle stigma around being care experienced. Shaunna is part of a feminist group which advocates for rights for women. She loves watching live music, being in nature and reading feminist literature.

https://www.linkedin.com/in/shaunna-devine/; https://twitter.com/ShaunnaDevine8; https://somaffect.org/people/sdevine/.

Siani is happily divorced and remarried, with 3 kids, 2 cats and 2 dogs. She runs her own business, giving digital support to mainly education/wellbeing businesses. Siani volunteers with text crisis service Women's Aid and Shout, and runs support organisations for local parents as well, which she set up after having her first daughter in 2013. In her spare time she loves gardening, being creative, reading, yoga and walking.

Tim is the Director of T-Junction Children's Services, set up in 2016 as a direct response to having worked in the sector for many years. Tim knew that residential homes could be outstanding, and he leads the way. Alongside running three homes, Tim shares his expertise through his other company, Tim Clare Consultancy, training for therapeutic care.

Tim is an individual who has lived and breathed the care system. He was in care himself for 20 years. Since leaving care, he has made it his mission to improve services and outcomes for children in care in a variety of job roles.

Tim has acquired many qualifications on his journey, and has also carried out his own research on the effects of how being placed into the 'care' of local authorities (foster care, residential care and so on) affects an individual's educational achievement and the likelihood that young people placed in such care will then engage in criminal activity.

Tim hopes to one day write and publish his own book, and fully intends to inspire and motivate those working with children in care with the messages he gives. Tim hopes to share past experiences in the hope this will lead to more positive experiences for those young people who come into care through no fault of their own.

Whilst everyone was invited to contribute a biography, not everyone wanted to.

Care Home Flickerings

Searching
for unconditional love,
away from horrors
of night time wanderings;
boys and girls looking
for comfort in
all the wrong places.

Pushing,
fighting a slow death,
one mosaic piece at a
time, wide eyed wondering
if someone would pick
them to return home.

Waiting,
a pointless game, the
years formed walls
cemented by the carelessness
of society's
throw away remarks.
you turned out alright considering…

Chrissy Kelly

DOI: 10.4324/9781003257967-1

PART ONE

DOI: 10.4324/9781003257967-2

3

Introduction

It is said that we all have a book within us, and I learnt that I am no exception. I sat for months, if not years, with the burning desire to write a book. I have always felt that I was an author: an unpublished writer who found great relief upon discovering blogging in 2009. From that moment I wrote about everything, absolutely everything – every pain, every joy, every misunderstood emotion.

Blogging is where this all really began. The pleasure, relief and cathartic healing that overcame me are what allowed me to believe that I could bring together an entire book! For a long time I had felt that I had many stories to tell, stories that would heal the wounds left over from years of therapeutic interventions; stories about life attending a 12-step programme and the journey through self-help books galore and, ultimately, stories that would help others. I have learnt that I need to share my stories with others, and I need the space to do so in a non-judgemental, supportive place. I have learnt that we will mostly benefit from telling our stories, and I have learnt that I have *only* found benefit in telling my stories. When we stand up and stand out and share our story we also open up the possibility of helping another person make sense of their own story too. However, we must own our own stories. They are not within us to be coerced from us before we have truly understood that they belong to us.

The impetus for this book was a desire to write something more autobiographical, something more about what shapes us as adults and what we are left to deal with and heal and recover from. I was in care

DOI: 10.4324/9781003257967-3

for part of my childhood, and I spent many years learning to deal with the aftermath of my experience predominately alone. When I first wrote this book in 2013, I was deeply aware of the silence of the voices of adults who were in care. Talking to people without this experience was something I had learnt to avoid as it had mostly been greeted with disbelief, pity or a genuine lack of interest. At that time I didn't really know other adults who had had the same experiences that I had. I rarely met a person who had been in care as a child in a personal capacity. Times have changed profoundly, and social media has ensured that there are a variety of groups, collectives, writing and art that can be accessed 24 hours a day from a small handheld device!

This book was the first time that I said out loud how I felt about what happened to me. This naturally drew me to thinking about other people with these experiences, and I wanted to find them and share their stories too. The voices of adults who were once in care, and where life has taken them, strike me as still being tokenistic, deemed irrelevant and lost in narratives that are heavily tied up with administrative data that consistently focuses on 'poor outcomes'.

This administrative data collected annually by the UK's Department for Education lacks any nuance about life in care, or indeed about what happens after care. It is not designed to be nuanced. It is not designed to capture, for example, how it 'feels' to be a child in care and how those feelings continue to affect children long into adulthood. Through the stories in this book, I intend to shed some light on the lived aspect of being in care, and I hope that this may somehow influence the reader. If you are a policy maker, consider this to be knowledge for informing and shaping good practice. If you are working or living with children or young people who are in care or on the edge of care, then use this book to add to your skills. If you have been in care, enjoy the connection. If you are finding out about the care experience for the first time, enjoy being privy to knowledge that is so often hidden, unspoken of and buried.

No one experience is the same. I have never heard my story repeated or two stories told as the same. We are all unique. However, there are things about the care experience that are unique, such as its bureaucratic nature; that every adult around you is paid to be there; that you attend large, often intimidating, meetings; and that your every move, especially negative ones, will be written up in a file that will be kept in the possession of others. This is a document which can often be thought of as an interesting read about where others are at in their career rather than the kind of information kept by parents. A file is not a record of the first step, first word, first giggle. Think more the first judgement, the first breakdown, the first unacceptable behaviour. Having lived and worked within the system, it can lend itself to practices that can be far from relational, far from trauma informed and far from the idea that relationships are therapeutic.

It was an interesting journey back in 2013, exploring the areas of my life that presented themselves for inclusion in the book. Sometimes my varied, complex life almost seems like it belongs to another. Other times it nestles in my diaphragm, clinging tightly to my solar plexus, weaving and interweaving between all my muscular fibres. Writing my story all those years ago brought me and my experiences closer together, so deeply that I was finally able to let them go. Reading everything I wrote again for this third edition mirrors to me that I feel a million miles away from the things that troubled me, the unspoken events, feelings and hurts. In that sense, it did its job. The deep imprint left by that part of my life has healed. That said, I am choosing to leave my story in here with very few amendments. It deserves to stay intact. As it was. In that moment of time from the place that I understood it. It will never be spoken of with such rawness as it was then, for I have changed. We all change. We adapt. We see the world as we are in that moment. Like a painting, it is entitled to remain as it was when written. Where legislation is referred to, I have brought that up to date for the reader's ease. In terms of policy, government and legislation shifts, we are a long way from where we were when I originally used data from the long-deceased Social Exclusion Unit.

The journey to writing this book started in a ground-floor room, a basic room on a beach in Lefkada, Greece. For a week I spent my mornings sitting on a little plastic chair working on a plastic table covered in fruit and bottled water on a very shabby terrace. The trees nearby served as 'poles' to tie string to, to provide the washing with somewhere to dry. Homeless, starving cats and gorgeous geckos whizzed past me every now and again. The sea was right in front of me, with its many shades like a tapestry of blue, not dissimilar to the green tapestry of the English countryside. Were I inclined, I could have thrown a stone into the water; it was that close. In that moment I acknowledged that I was exactly where I was meant to be. This perfect place – a place I had never been before, a place I had never even seen a picture of – is exactly the way it looked when I visualised myself writing at my laptop, being a writer.

It is important to say that the writing here represents the perspectives of the writers. These are our own stories, not those of anyone else. We all have different perceptions of events, traumas and consequences; and, as the reflections will show, those change over time in a multitude of ways.

So what is this book about? What is it for? What is its purpose?

It's not:

- a research project, so it is not written from a place of academic rigour
- a representative sample of the thousands of care experienced adults that I could have spoken to
- an interpretation of administrative data.
    It is:
    - a collection of voices, observing the nuances of each person's experiences
    - an exploration of some of the issues people have had to deal with across the life course
    - an insight to further understanding this aspect of a life lived.

Lots of people grow up facing all sorts of challenges that are taken into adulthood, but this book is about 'care' in the UK and the impact it has on children that is then carried with them throughout their lives. I also want to counterbalance the information out there regarding outcomes with some positive benefits that care leavers have taken from their experience.

Through the process of gathering the stories for this book I often felt as though I was looking in the mirror as I listened to the experiences of others. For while each story is so completely different, there are threads running through them all about the impact of being in care and what that has given us to deal with as adults, both positive and negative.

So, while this is not a piece of research, there are recurrent themes to be taken from here that can add to an understanding and a more compassionate approach towards the children that society undertakes to 'look after'.

I first wrote this book for me. I then wrote it for us. I am now writing this book for you.

1
1970–1980

I am more whole than I have ever been.
This book is brought to you from all of me: the child who
  has been in care,
the child who has been homeless, the recovering
  alcoholic,
the woman with a degree in Sociology,
the woman with an endless fascination for politics and
  society,
the mother of adult children, the person who worked in
  social work and education
the woman who has been on a self-development journey
  for over 30 years,
the lover of chocolate and coffee, the woman doing a
  PhD and the woman grappling with the menopause.
I offer it all. I am not to be placed in a box that can be
  ticked. After all – and I want you to really understand
  and believe this – none of us are …

This is a story about love and pain, hurt and isolation; a depth of a life,
the big things and the little things. We don't live our lives in theories
and philosophies; we live them through our relationships with others
and where we feel we reside within those relationships. It is how we
explain those relationships that enables us to tell our stories; and I tell

    DOI: 10.4324/9781003257967-4

mine through the language of emotion, through the feelings that I have been left with. For it is that which I will always remember: how I felt.

My whole arrival in the world seems to me to have been surrounded by shame. I think the fact that my mother had had sex at all was too much for my gran to bear. As far as I could tell, sex was an activity endured by a married woman in return for being looked after, for being housed. I remember my gran talking about the 'red cape' that she made my mother wear to 'hide the baby', and I remember thinking, "That's me. I'm the baby. Why would you want to hide me?" I only know what I have been told, the stories changing through the passage of time and the storytellers and, of course, through their own journeys of understanding. The rest of what I know is the emotional imprint left upon my soul and in my cells which have taken, and continue to take, a long journey of recovery and healing.

So it's 1969, and, as I understand it, my mother had been 'dating' someone for a few months, maybe three. His name has always been a mystery, but Dave and Fred have been mentioned on the various occasions that I have tried to have a conversation about who this mystery person – my father – may be. A night out in Wigan, a few drinks, and a gullible and possibly sheltered and vulnerable 20-year-old girl became a recipe for disaster. The young woman has a good night out and then pays the price forever, as on this night I am conceived.

The backdrop for my first ten years is Southport, a northern town near Manchester and Liverpool, filled with beautiful Victorian architecture and gaudy ice cream parlours selling Knickerbocker Glories, the ultimate dessert of the 1970s' seaside resort.

Lord Street carries the air of a shopping street to savour, with its Victorian arcades, its closeness to the seafront and the large buildings competing for appreciation. I doubt it was a very forward-thinking town in 1969, and being a teenager here may well have been quite stifling, especially knowing that in other parts of the country there was a revolution going on, a complete shift into another generation and alleged sexual freedoms. The North West of England was potentially still not quite ready to deal with diversity, women's liberation and, of course, birth outside marriage.

I seem to remember my gran telling me that one day 'he' (the man I believe to be my dad) came to our house in Zetland Street. It was a three-bedroom semi-detached Victorian house; a lovely house with a garden that, to my child's eye, seemingly went on forever. He was told at the door that I had been aborted, terminated, removed – whatever terminology you find comfortable. My French granny had told me this in her incredibly clumsy way. She was often emotionally clumsy and had a bluntness with words due to English being her second language.

Emotional articulation wasn't part of her communication, not appropriate in her generation at all, so translating a feeling into words was always going to lead to the strangest and most insensitive of exchanges. I was always uncomfortable about the fact that I knew this piece of information, this knowledge of hiding me, aborting me, removing me – the very nature of such a discussion serving to give out a whole multitude of messages. Not being wanted and the stories that surrounded this truth created self-loathing that I had to crawl my way out of. I would have been about 12, maybe 13, when I found out about the abortion conversation. Even then I was very aware that this was knowledge I really ought not to have and that I may hold on to forever – and indeed I have.

I don't believe that knowledge like this is a good thing for a child, for a teenager or for a woman, but it is information that I have nonetheless; and, in the emptiness of the knowledge available to me, I attempt gratitude. What I have taken from this, and what has sat in my 'emotional database', is that someone else removed my right to know my father. Not only would it be logistically a piece of magic for me to find him, but he will never search for me as he does not know I am here; and, my goodness, did I spend my teenage years shouting "I AM HERE!"

When people first learn of this aspect of my history, I am often asked, "Have you tried to find him?", "Do you want to find him?" or "Are you upset about it?" I have had intense periods of searching, intense periods of anger and intensely overwhelming emotions of loss. The unfaltering sensation of loss and abandonment has tapped me on the shoulder throughout my entire life. I understand now that there have been endless scenarios where I have created loss and abandonment for myself to ensure repetition and certainty and some sort of strange familiarity, yet not knowing why and not knowing how to attract something else.

So here I was, the unwanted, born into one of the remaining homes for unmarried mothers after my gran had gone to the church for guidance – because in 1969 that was where you went for guidance. The shame must have wrapped itself around everyone like a blanket and stayed there as if we were in a permanent winter. It seems that there was some debate as to whether I would remain with my mother, and I spent the first few weeks of my life in foster care while decisions were made.

The indulgence of retrospect and reflection has cursed me from time to time as I have imagined what life might have been like if I had been adopted rather than returned to the house with my mother and my gran. Where those who were adopted think about what their lives may have been like if they'd stayed with their birth mother, mine was the other way round. Two sides of the same coin; two aspects of the same shadow.

My belief is that this early separation caused an irreparable amount of damage to our relationship. As a mother myself, I cannot imagine how I would have managed that. The biological urge to look after and protect and feed your baby is so powerful I think I could have killed a person who tried to take my baby from me.

However, I do think it's possible that the lost bonding between my mother and I could have been repaired through a positive trusting relationship; but our lack of emotional and physical connection and mutual understanding, and what I perceive as her difficulties with mothering in general, meant that we never recovered, and this has stayed with us to date.

For the most part, 1970s' Britain was not a place of emotional exploration, personal development and healing. The parents of the generation who were at this time becoming parents had been through a war, and the very nature of the horror of all that war entailed meant that many conversations were just not had.

With regard to parenting, this was a time when crying babies were put at the bottom of the garden in their prams to 'have a little sleep' and gripe water still contained 3.6 per cent alcohol. Parenting, it seems to me, sat in a cradle of "I know you can feel it, but let's pretend you can't."

Having said that, my gran was a mothering and capable woman who instilled a sense of female strength and a 'get on with it' attitude that was peppered with hugs and kisses. She was a great cook and seamstress, and held her head high even when it pained her to do so. Living in those times without a husband – he had died less than a decade into their marriage – and without hope of finding any kind of replacement, learning how to change a fuse in a plug was on the menu along with how to make a good roux for a cheese sauce. For my first ten years, within this strange triangle of women, Gran was the mother, I was the daughter and my mother was more like an older sister.

The Soundtrack

Tie a Yellow Ribbon – Tony Orlando and Dawn
Jeans On – David Dundas
Mamma Mia – Abba
Under the Moon of Love – Showaddywaddy
Bye Bye Baby – Bay City Rollers

The Headlines

Miners' strikes
The Winter of Discontent
Elvis Presley dies
Thatcher Thatcher Milk Snatcher
The IRA

The TV

Coronation Street
Charlie's Angels
Doctor Who
The Generation Game
Jim'll Fix It (the irony is not to be lost on the UK reader)

Remembered Moments

Being Collected from Nursery

It's sometime in the early 1970s when I first became aware that I was supposed to have a dad. I was at nursery or primary school, I can't remember which, and my uncle, my mother's brother, was visiting once and came to collect me. My uncle has always remained in my life, and while there have been difficult periods of time, our relationship has continued to be a constant and I have always valued it. In my younger days I naturally felt abandoned by him too. Why didn't he come and rescue me? Why did he let me go into care? Why did he not do something?

I remember the conversation on that walk home with him as if it were yesterday. The content of the conversation is vivid; the date isn't. Somebody – another child – said to me, "Is that your dad?" "No, silly," I replied, "he's my uncle!" The words were spoken out of the mouth of a babe as if it were far more 'normal' to have an uncle collecting you from school than a father. This triggered some internal questioning: why don't I have a dad?

It must have been around this time that I asked my mother this question, to which she replied: "He was killed … in a plane crash." "Oh," I said. So my dad was dead. I didn't need to concern myself with the minutiae of his lack of presence because he had died while I was playing with my Sindy doll and nobody had thought to mention it before.

It was many years later, through a violent row with my mother in my screaming adolescence, that I was informed that this was an untruth. Another piece of puzzling information: it's deemed ok to say that he's dead but not to tell me what his name is … Yet another conundrum that plagued me for many years and that I was unable to resolve.

Reflection

My gran was my greatest buffer from adversity. She was a woman of her time, born in 1911, placing her firmly as a developing child in the First World War and a young woman in the Second. My view now is not so much that she was unable to articulate emotion, but rather that she was in fact incredibly emotionally nurturing considering her life experiences, and she undoubtedly struggled to make sense of the breakdown of my relationship with my mother, her daughter.

Without her, my life would have been very different. A baby's brain has around 100 billion neurons and we wire up our internal architecture through our physical environment and our social environment in relationship with our carers (Barrett, 2021). I wired up in my early years with her adoring love, consistent care and continued presence. When we talk about relational buffering (Perry & Dobson, 2010) we're talking about the capacity to recover *because* of our relationships. Even though I was born in a mother and baby unit and had my first vital weeks away from my carers – my mother and my gran – the warmth and nurture from my gran, coupled with an intergenerational 'knowing' of my carer, supported my development in ways that I could, and have, carried into adulthood.

Discussion Points

What early buffering relationships supported your development?

What potential impact do you think may occur with the early removal of a baby from their carers?

What considerations have you given to intergenerational trauma in your personal journey and/or in your professional work?

References

Barrett, F.L. (2021). *Seven and a Half Lessons About the Brain*. Pan Macmillan, Basingstoke.

Perry, B.D. & Dobson, C. (2010). The role of healthy relational interactions in buffering the impact of childhood trauma. In Gil, E. (Ed.) *Working with Children to Heal Interpersonal Trauma: The Power of Play*. Guilford Press, New York.

2
1980–1983

In 1980, everything changed. I honestly believe that my gran and my mother did the best they could with the information they had at the time. I had gone to all sorts of extracurricular activities before it was popular to do so and deemed by society as a prerequisite to 'good' parenting. Money was tight, but it was found to give me dance classes, piano lessons and the Brownies. In this regard I was privileged, I suppose; but the emotional 'neglect', lies and secrecy were starting to take their toll on my own development.

My need for intellectual, emotional and physical stimulation was beyond challenging, especially for my mother. The bridge between what I needed and what she could provide was too big to cross. I believe I was neglected in this way, but I do not say that with any blame attached to it. When we have children we have to deal with what they bring us. But there was no acceptance back then of me, just as I came – as an individual with my own wishes, wants, hope and desires; and because that was not shown to me, I became unable to show that to my mother. As much as she couldn't accept me she taught me, by default, not to accept her – I was unacceptable and so was she. This dynamic has plagued our relationship for decades.

This complex interplay of a triangle-shaped dynamic that lacked honesty and authenticity, along with the underpinning of non-acceptance of who we all were and how that had been manifested through this 'unwanted pregnancy', meant that by the age of ten I was already a complex and misunderstood little girl. My emotional needs had not

    DOI: 10.4324/9781003257967-5

really been met, and I had grown up in an environment filled with shame – Catholic shame, Victorian shame and women's shame.

My social skills were a little odd, reflecting my home environment, and I had few friends. Saying all of that, it's possible that I would not have become such a damaged teenager had my circumstances not been about to change. It's just another reflection among the many about what might or might not have been. Who knows? Life throws so many things at us, other people create situations for us, and we learn to live with the fact that we will never know any outcome other than the one we experience.

As an adult, I can choose how I view the world. I can reframe everything if I want to, and I can understand that all of the experiences I had made me who I am today. If I so wish, I can be deeply grateful to my mother and my gran for their flaws, and also to the father who arrived that day at the front door in Zetland Street and failed to check if I really was 'aborted' – and so it goes on. But I cannot do that as a child, as a dependant, as a vulnerable human being.

For my mother, the inevitable search for a suitable mate was ongoing. It's a search I can understand as a woman and as a mother, but it made little sense to me as a child. I think they met through an advert. I'm not sure of the details and I have never asked. The marriage only lasted a few months, maybe a year, yet I have some of my most vivid memories from that time – actual memories and emotional imprints of feelings felt and fear created. I think they dated for about a year before they got married, though I don't recall them seeing each other that many times. In our beautiful seaside town, Southport, people had a 'baath'; he lived with his two daughters on a road to nowhere in a small town in Northamptonshire that I came to loathe, where the people had a 'barth'.

I particularly remember one of these visits. The incident is not a new memory; that is, I have recalled it many times over the years, examining it over and over, searching for information in a plea to make sense of it. I would have been about nine years old and my mother was almost crying, saying she couldn't carry her suitcase any longer as it was hurting her hands. We were changing trains at Rugby on our way to the place of 'barth', or on our way back – I don't recall. We had to walk over a footbridge to get to the right platform and I took responsibility, both emotionally and physically, for my mother's hurting hands and her suitcase. I carried the suitcase. I don't know how long I carried the case for. It may not have been long at all; but, nevertheless, I was the adult carrying the heavy suitcase, an analogy I can safely use about behaviour through my teenage years and a good part of my adulthood. I am the adult. I am alone. I don't need you. I don't need anyone. I can manage, thank you very much. The impact that had on my relationships was an obvious one.

It's strange how some memories are new ones, wandering around our thinking space until we are shocked by their appearance; and then there are other memories, ones we have visited so many times. And then there are the memories that are buried so deep that even a song, a smell or a photograph won't bring them to the fore. Yet we know that they're there somewhere, trapped in our emotional imprint.

I have spent time thinking about this in my adult life. This scene of a nine-year-old girl clutching a suitcase that must have been nearly as big as her features in my memory bank with such clarity. It has helped me understand my inability to be looked after in my relationships (until I was confronted with this in a short marriage), my overdeveloped sense of responsibility to just about everyone and a tendency to want to make sure everyone else is alright before myself. I have worked through a lot of this, through understanding it and relearning new responses and behaviours; but my early adulthood was plagued with it all.

It is within this context that the absence of a father has felt so pronounced, and it is in this place that I have craved being looked after and taken care of in a healthy way, in that way that a father does.

The short marriage of my mother and the man from the advert was a disaster, lasting less than a year. It was fuelled by poor communication, anger, hurt and completely mismanaged expectations. I cannot speak for the adults; I can only surmise with adult eyes, observing through the memories of a child. But I suspect that he needed a mother for his children and my mother needed a husband. The three children, thrown together in this unlikely family, were not consulted on this. It was 1980 and emotional literacy, living consciously and listening to children were not part of popular culture. *Psychology* magazine was yet to be on the shelves, and I believe that it is in this setting that I felt the most emotionally neglected.

This period of time was a huge turning point for me. I felt so badly the loss of my gran, who had mothered me for ten years and remained in Southport. If I had felt as though I was different to everyone else through living with two women, one of whom was French, I certainly felt different in this place. All of a sudden I had a dad and two sisters, Sharon and Sarah – more children experiencing more outcomes from the strange decisions taken by the adults in their lives. I was now in a step-family, a completely new family with their own way of living and expectations and set of norms and values. I felt completely alone and isolated and abandoned and misunderstood; and yet no one ever spoke to me about how I was feeling. Nobody said a word.

New School – September 1981

I bumbled my way through the final year of primary school in this new town in the depths of Northamptonshire with the words "Why can't you just fit in?" ringing through my ears. It was my mother's favourite sentence for a number of years. This was quickly followed by my entry into secondary school. My first secondary school was an all-girls' school and I was in the top set for most subjects. Academically bright yet emotionally distressed, I was sharing my space with the children who lived in nice houses, with mums and dads and perceived harmony. It was here that I learnt the art of fantasising about other people's lives. In my little fantasy world they were all loved and cared for and listened to and understood; and, being a child, I just felt jealous, painfully jealous.

My behaviour deteriorated pretty quickly. I was angry and destructive, and was screaming externally and internally for someone to help me and listen to what was happening for me. Drinking and drugging commenced, and my inner turmoil spilled out into just about any room I entered. At school things were so bad that I spent most of my lessons in the music room on my own, and I knew that the other children were told, "If you don't behave, you'll end up like Lisa Cherry" – yes, you'll end up abandoned, lost and in the music room too!

My early teenage years felt cruel and lonely. I was plagued by all the usual teenage angst alongside the imbalance and instability that sits on top of living in a volatile home. The arguments between my mother and I were shocking, sometimes physical and always loudly verbal.

The manifestation of the previous 12 or so years of silenced emotion and unspoken truths exploded from within me like a tornado. This was the beginning of all that was destructive and it arrived without warning, horrifying those around me. Every piece of self-loathing behaviour stood up and made itself known. This burst of loud expression, coupled with my social ineptitude, meant that my friendships were complicated and I learnt quickly how to ensure alienation and rejection. I went from being described as incredibly "bright and promising" to "Lisa will never make much of herself." But the unobserved tragedy was that I had far bigger problems to deal with than that!

The discovery of my sexuality, which is daunting enough for any teenager, left me in undesirable and risky situations as I searched for someone to look after me and to protect me from myself.

As an adult, with many years on a healing journey under my belt alongside years working extensively with young people in equal and further distress than I experienced myself, I understand this behaviour all too well. In my search for that place of approval, of belonging, of acceptance and for someone to take care of me, I found myself in many a dark place.

Abusers, paedophiles, child traffickers, drug dealers; they know exactly where to look and what 'qualities' a child has to have in order to be 'groomed'. I am convinced today that I escaped so much because I screamed so loudly and was usually a liability to the most sophisticated abuser. I was vulnerable, oh yes, but in a loud, angry way that served me as a great protection. I have worked with many other young people, male and female, who were less fortunate and there continues to be a lucrative market in the use of vulnerable, lost children, whether they are 'in care' or not.

Here is a brief overview of Acts in place to protect children and how inquiries have led to changes in legislation – and yet there is still a mountain to climb when protecting vulnerable children and young people.

> **The Children and Young Persons Act 1933**: one of the older pieces of child protection legislation. It includes the list of offences against children that continue to be referred to as Schedule One offences.
>
> **The Children Act 1989**: This forms the basis for the current child protection system. At the time, it was hailed by the then Lord Chancellor, Lord Mackay of Clashfern, as "the most comprehensive and far-reaching reform of child law which has come before Parliament in living memory".
>
> **The United Nations Convention on the Rights of the Child 1989**: ratified by the UK on 16 December 1991.
>
> **The Human Rights Act 1998**: This isn't specifically about the rights of children, but they are covered by this as they have rights as humans in the eyes of the law.
>
> **Children's Commissioner for Wales Act 2001**: created the first children's commissioner post in the UK. The principal aim of the Commissioner is to safeguard and promote the rights and welfare of children. Subsequent legislation created a children's commissioner for Northern Ireland (the Commissioner for Children and Young People (NI) Order 2003), Scotland (Commissioner for Children and Young People (Scotland) Act 2003) and England (sections 1–9 of the Children Act 2004).

The English Commissioner is unique in the UK in not having the remit to promote children's rights.

The Education Act 2002: This specifies the requirement for school governing bodies, Local Education Authorities/LEAs (which we no longer have) and further education (FE) institutions to safeguard and promote the welfare of children.

Section 120 of the Adoption and Children Act 2002: amends the Children Act 1989 by expanding the definition of 'harm' to include witnessing domestic violence.

The Sexual Offences Act 2003 was introduced to update the legislation relating to offences against children. It includes the offences of grooming, abuse of position of trust and trafficking, and covers offences committed by UK citizens whilst abroad.

The Female Genital Mutilation Act 2003 extends the existing legislation criminalising female genital mutilation in the UK by making it an offence for UK nationals or permanent UK residents to take a girl abroad, or to help others to take a girl abroad, to carry out female genital mutilation, even in countries where the practice is legal.

The Domestic Violence, Crime and Victims Act 2004: closes a legal loophole (whereby defendants in murder and manslaughter cases could escape conviction by claiming each other had killed the child) by creating a new offence of causing or allowing the death of a child or vulnerable adult. The offence establishes a new criminal responsibility for members of a household where they know that a child or vulnerable adult is at significant risk of serious harm.

Children Act 2004: Following the death of eight-year-old Victoria Climbié in 2000, the government asked Lord Laming to conduct an inquiry to help decide whether it needed to introduce new legislation and guidance to improve the child protection system in England. The government's response to the *Victoria Climbié Inquiry* report (Laming, 2003) was the

Department for Education and Skills *Keeping Children Safe* report (DfES, 2003) and the *Every Child Matters* green paper (Great Britain Parliament, 2003), which in turn led to the Children Act 2004.

Although much of this legislation still applies, the election of a Conservative/Liberal Democrat coalition government in May 2010 led to a shift in thinking on child protection, and a number of changes in approach came under discussion.

The Children and Adoption Act 2006: gives courts more flexible powers to facilitate child contact and enforce contact orders when separated parents are in dispute.

The Children and Young Persons Act 2008: legislates for the recommendations in the *Care Matters* white paper (DfES, 2007) to provide high-quality care and services for children in care. It covers England and Wales (in part) and also places a duty on registrars to notify the Local Safeguarding Children Board of all child deaths.

The Borders, Citizenship and Immigration Act 2009 places a duty on the UK Border Agency to safeguard and promote children's welfare (section 55), bringing them in line with other public bodies that have contact with children.

The Apprenticeships, Skills, Children and Learning Act 2009 legislates for there to be two lay members from the local community sitting on each Local Safeguarding Children Board. The government later repealed some of the other provisions in this Act, including the requirement to draw up Children and Young People's Plans, and withdrew related statutory children's trust guidance.

The Education Act 2011 makes changes to provisions on school discipline and places restrictions on the public reporting of allegations made against teachers.

The Domestic Violence, Crime and Victims (Amendment) Act 2012 extends the 2004 offence to include "causing or allowing a child or vulnerable adult to suffer serious physical harm".

The Protection of Freedoms Act was passed on 1 May 2012. Following the 2002 murders of ten-year-olds Jessica Chapman and Holly Wells, the Bichard Inquiry (Bichard, 2004) examined vetting procedures. The government's response was the Safeguarding Vulnerable Groups Act 2006, which established a new centralised vetting and barring scheme for people working with children. Following a 2011 review of this scheme, the Protection of Freedoms Act saw the replacement of the vetting and barring scheme with a new, scaled-back disclosure and barring service focusing only on roles involving working most closely with vulnerable groups.

The Children and Social Work Act 2017 sets out corporate parenting principles and the safeguarding of children among other areas of concern, including professional standards in social work.

Since the National Society for the Prevention of Cruelty to Children (NSPCC) was founded in 1884 it has played a key role in influencing and drafting legislation to protect children.

The history of protecting children is relatively new and *how* we do it is a continuing debate between politicians, policy makers and media representation, intensified on the back of neglect, death and public outrage.

*

Real change comes when all professionals and carers in children's lives are given the emotional intelligence training to understand how to be emotionally available and connected to the young people in their care. They also need the time and space to deliver their services effectively alongside the opportunity to explore their own personal development, thus enabling them to treat children as individuals rather than trying to fit people into categories and boxes where none exist.

Until that is at the heart of practice, the level of 'care', protection and attention children receive will remain a lottery dependent on the practitioner as opposed to the service itself. Everyone I spoke to had examples and experiences that reflected prejudice and social exclusion.

The Soundtrack

Ant Music – Adam and the Ants
Just Can't Get Enough – Depeche Mode
One in Ten – UB40
Going Underground – The Jam
It Ain't What You Do – Fun Boy Three and Bananarama

The Headlines

Royal wedding
Yorkshire Ripper
The Falklands
John Lennon is assassinated

The TV

Dallas
Kenny Everett
Grange Hill
Private Benjamin
The A-Team

Remembered Moments

The Glass Door 1978

I'm coming home from Brownies I think and I've been dropped off outside or collected and brought home, I can't recall. It must be cold and it's definitely dark, and I just want to get inside. It might even have been raining. We had a porch on our semi-detached house in Zetland Street, a posh porch that my Gran had had specially built with a lovely half-glass door. As I ran up to the house from the car that dropped me off I used the palm of my hand to push the door open as I thought it was just pulled to, but it was locked shut and my hand went straight through the glass.

There was blood everywhere. I remember my gran and my mother being very angry as I had broken the glass. The bandaging of my wrist was done with an angry, fierce pulling and pushing and huffing and puffing. I didn't mean it, really I didn't, I'm sorry, I'm hurting. For whatever reason, it seemed to me, the glass door was far more important. The scar on my wrist is just barely visible, but remains with me – as with all scars.

Reflection

I have since raised my own children into adulthood, and that process has altered my perspectives far more profoundly than I could ever have imagined. We arrive in the world with our unique DNA, the experiences we have in the womb, the labour that we are birthed with, the capacity of our caregivers, the community around us and the political temperature towards children and families manifested in government policy; and then, every experience we have within that relational context. This makes our development unique, complex and something that can never be replicated. We are each built in moments in time interacting with this physical and social environment. Watching the impact of that development in your own children is confronting, beautiful and potentially quite sad because, as a parent, we have to come to terms with the fact that there are things we simply cannot change, cannot control and cannot always mitigate. I always thought that love would be enough; but my view now would be that love isn't always enough but it is all we really have, so love love love.

Understanding all of that changed the way I understand my mother, what happened to her and what happened to me. I don't believe that we will ever fully recover from the history we have between us, but we manage each other far better than I thought possible. I feel much more kindly about the empathic failures and misattunements that haunted the relationship between us. Even when we're not doing very well at all, we really are doing our best. Reflecting on how differently I see certain things reminds me of the quote "We do not see things as they are. We see things as we are."[1]

Discussion Points

What role does a school have that can make a difference for a child in care?

What qualities might a teacher have that would make them a buffering relationship?

What does protecting children and young people mean to you, and how do you take responsibility for doing so?

Note

1 Rabbi Shemuel ben Nachmani, as quoted in the Talmudic tractate Berakhot (55b).

References

Bichard, M. (2004). *Return to an Address of the Honourable the House of Commons Dated 22nd June 2004 for the Bichard Inquiry Report* (HC 2003-04 653). London: Stationery Office.

DfES (2003). *Keeping Children Safe: The Government's Response to the 'Victoria Climbié Inquiry' Report and Joint Chief Inspector's Report 'Safeguarding Children'* (Cm 5861). London: Stationery Office.

DfES (2007). *Care Matters: Time for Change.* Norwich: HMSO.

Great Britain Parliament (2003). *Every Child Matters.* London: Stationery Office.

Laming, H. (2003). *The Victoria Climbié Inquiry: Report of an Inquiry by Lord Laming* (Cm. 5730). London: Stationery Office.

3

1983

It's August 1983 and I am about to enter a system, a system that will protect me and give me and my mother much needed time apart. We had no family meetings, no discussions, no therapy, no group work. I don't remember any intervention or support offered to help my mother be a mother or help me with my emotional turmoil. No. I just remember being asked if I wanted to go and stay with another family for a few months so we could have a break.

All that happened in those first six months of being in care was that my teenage anger became firmly rooted, leaving me with no desire to speak to my mother again. Prior to leaving the rows had become more violent, and nothing would have changed as no work was ever done to try and change anything. I arrived in care with all of these difficult unanswered questions fuelled by emotional starvation, and the system did not help me try and improve things, make anything better, help me heal and grow and thrive. Rather it gave me the experience of 'care' in the 1980s, which was swiftly followed by the inevitable bout of home-lessness and all of the risks and damage that accompanied the whole experience. I couldn't help feeling that it was somehow all a bit of an accident: a series of events where no one tried to intervene – events that I should never have taken part in.

I have never seen my files, so I will never know whether my rec-ollection is correct. I have never had the desire to read emotionless statements and perceptions from the myriad of different social workers I had during my four-year 'care' experience.

DOI: 10.4324/9781003257967-6

But I remember that day, the day I became a child 'in care'. I'm 13 years old, and it is a stifling hot day in August 1983 and the social worker is collecting me from the flat my mother and I live in. I think the person was a woman but I can't remember. They are there to take me to my foster parents for six months – a temporary placement giving my mother and me some space, apparently. I remember very little about how this situation even came about. How do social services even know about me? If it had been known what being in care was going to do to me and what harsh experiences it would give me, would whoever alerted social services have started this road of destruction for me?

Who Is in Care?

According to the Department for Education (2020a), in England there were 80,080 looked after children at 31 March 2020, a number which has increased from 64,400 since March 2010:

- 72 per cent of children in care lived in foster care.
- 3 per cent of children in care were placed for adoption.
- 13 per cent of children in care lived in secure units, children's homes and semi-independent accommodation.
- 3 per cent of children in care lived in the community, independently or in residential employment.
- 7 per cent of children in care were placed with their parent(s). This may be because the parent(s) consented to their child receiving care from the local authority, under an arrangement known as voluntary accommodation.

Have things changed, I wonder? I think it unlikely that I would end up in care in the current climate, and I know that a lot more preventative work goes on today than ever did back in the 1980s. It's hard for me not to wonder what might have happened to me had I not been steered into that place.

There has been enough research to show that being in care can lead to all sorts of entries into other systems, such as the mental health system and the prison system, and that homelessness, teenage pregnancy and lack of education are areas of concern and have a high proportion of those with a care background contained in their statistics. Let us not forget that beyond each one of those numbers is a person.

Administrative data collected on educational outcomes show the following:

- Looked after children are almost four times more likely to have a special educational need (SEN) than other children, and are almost nine times more likely to have an education, health and care (EHC) plan than other children.
- In 2019, 52 per cent of looked after children reached expected standards in reading, 43 per cent in writing, 49 per cent in maths and 60 per cent in science. Compared to non-looked after children, attainment for looked after children is much lower.
- In 2019, 37 per cent of looked after children reached the expected standard in the headline measure reading, writing and maths when assessed at the end of Year 6 (around age 11).
- At Key Stage 4 (ages 14–16) the average Attainment 8 score for looked after children and children in need is much lower than for non-looked after children (Department for Education, 2020b).

Other Impacts on Future Life – Findings from the Looked-after Children Grown Up (LACGro) Project, 2021

- Early death rates rose from being 40 per cent higher in 1971 to 360 per cent higher in 2001 for adults who had spent time in care.
- Mental health was consistently worse for children in care.
- The British data indicated that those who had been in care had lower qualifications, were more likely to be unemployed or out

of the labour force, more often had children and were teenage parents, were twice as likely to have depression, and that occurrences of homelessness and being on benefits were higher (Sacker et al., 2021).

There are many other statistics I could add here, statistics that highlight poor and negative outcomes, but I am choosing not to do that. One of the beautiful aspects of the stories in this book is that there are many ways to live after spending time in care, and one of them is to remain hidden, assimilating into society without being noticed at all. The spectrum is broad, and to linger on negative outcomes outside of policy making is to risk perpetuating narratives that do not serve us and actively seek to hinder.

*

I'm cursing and swearing and throwing all my clothes into a bag. I empty my mother's piggy bank to buy cigarettes, and I venomously shout around the flat that we shared together with an anger that can only be born out of sheer frustration, disappointment and hurt. She has failed in her ability to mother me and I have failed in my ability to be mothered by her. I am out of control. I smoke, I drink endless Woodpecker cider that I occasionally mix with spirits to ensure complete collapse, I like marijuana, I am just about to be excluded from my first school, I shoplift endlessly, my best friend has disappeared. I like Terry Hall, John Lennon, Sting and UB40. I eat rubbish, I say fuck a lot and I want to be loved. I want someone to hold me and stop this insanity that I am embarking upon. I am just a child.

*

I had many social workers, so it would be impossible to recall the names of more than a couple. One was a man who I liked and he gave me his cigarettes to smoke – a winner for any smoking teenager wanting to feel heard and vaguely important. Smoking was a real tool for me to be angry and for social workers to 'befriend' me. I recognised the latter and exploited it to the max!

The other one I remember was a woman called Eunice who was allocated to me (or was I allocated to her)? Eunice was my social worker for about 18 months when I was around 15 or 16 years old, although for some of that time she was on maternity leave and for some of that I had removed myself from the county. In essence, I knew her for about six months. She had a very cuddly appearance and drove a nice car, and I always felt that she liked me more than she was meant to. I remember that feeling a lot. It was a feeling that people wanted to help or assist or 'like' me but that it wasn't allowed or appropriate, or indeed relevant, for the reality is that I belonged to no one and was not the responsibility of another soul really. When that initially penetrated through the core of my being and the ability to articulate it made it real, it was a realisation that I carried as a ton of weight like a sack of stones.

The beauty of a sack of stones is that I learnt to take the stones out one by one: put the sack down, throw a stone away; put the sack down, throw one away. It is my sack of stones, I learnt, but I really don't have to carry it.

So, with regard to who collected me, I really can't recall what their name was or what they said. I was told that I was going to stay with foster parents for a break. What that actually meant was never clear and it all felt like a bit of a surprise. What sort of a family would they be? How would they live? No mention was made of what food they ate, what conversations they would have, what my room might be like; I just seem to remember arriving at a house.

It turned out to be a three-bed, 1930s' semi, the 'two double beds and a box' type of house. There was a very nice car in the drive, and I seemed to be meeting a 'family'. There was a mum, a dad and one, two, three children under five. Yuk! I could never quite fathom why they might want an angry teenager in the house with a workload like that, but I suspect they were misguided and possibly thought I might be helpful around the home and the children.

Useful tip: Teenagers are not helpful. Teenagers are not something that you have around the house through choice. I've never heard anyone say, "Shall we invite some teenagers round for dinner, darling, for some stimulating conversation and helpfulness?" No. And angry dysfunctional teenagers are even less helpful. This particular breed of adolescent wants to destroy everything in a sort of emotional 'quantitative easing' to reduce the sensation of pain. Did nobody mention that in the training manual for foster carers?

These poor people must have been as shocked as I was at my arrival into their already busy and chaotic family home.

I don't have many memories of this six-month union apart from collecting more knowledge that informed me that I was different, that I didn't 'fit in' and that I ought to be rejected back into the hands of the nameless social workers who would be able to offer another place of containment until I could be forgotten after the age of 16. I wonder, though, how many of us would be able to live in any family plucked at random and just happen to eat like they do, have sleeping patterns like they have and share their life values? I mean, really, how many? It's a tall order, isn't it? Especially for a child who has been on the kind of journey that got them there in the first place.

They were, to all intents and purposes, a hardworking, middle-class family trying to make a good life for their children. Every night we had a lovely big dinner with roast potatoes and vegetables, and my washing was done.

The dad, Phil, worked in sales I think, and the nice car in the drive that I had clocked upon arrival turned out to be a top-of-the-range Austin Maestro, which, at the time, was akin to something that might be used for space travel. I had never seen anything like it. It was dark blue, had lots of buttons and a dashboard like a fruit machine. It would look like the oldest car ever now, but back then it was impressive. He provided for his family and worked hard; and it was, I would say, my first real experience of what having a man in the house might look like when it was a happy family – and I yearned for it. I had never lived with it before, only glimpsing it through school friends' doorways or through listening in on conversations about how people lived.

My lack of actual knowledge, coupled with the curiosity of a teenager about how everyone else lives, started the process of feeding the fantasy that I had created about families: namely that they are wonderful, functional, loving environments where you are loved and all your needs are met forever and ever – and I didn't have one, and I wanted one!! Of course my adult eyes soon started to see the world as it actually was rather than how I wanted it to be. The fantasy barely persisted past a short burst of sighs around Christmas time as I watched the fantasy world that the media portrayed through its marketing material.

During my stay, my behaviour became more and more erratic as my ability to express myself was a voice left unheard. I took to walking everywhere barefoot – to town, to the shops, to everywhere. The reaction this generated supported my need to be seen. Without the skills of the adults around me to help me translate what I was feeling into something articulated, and therefore manageable, the spiral into self-destruction took a firm hold. Rejection came quickly and easily, and the next foster home awaited me.

The Soundtrack

Red Red Wine – UB40
Billie Jean – Michael Jackson
I Hear a Symphony – Diana Ross and the Supremes
Do They Know It's Christmas? – Band Aid
True – Spandau Ballet

The Headlines

Tommy Cooper dies
Strike action in the coal mining industry

1983

Prince William born
Unemployment is over 3 million
Neil Kinnock becomes leader of the Labour Party

The TV

Torvill and Dean performing Bolero
Happy Days
Knight Rider
Sons and Daughters
Brookside

Remembered Moments

Arriving in the Car

I'm working as a residential social worker. It's the early 1990s and I'm studying for a degree and supporting myself by being back in the very places I couldn't wait to leave: children's homes.

We have a new boy coming this morning and he's just arrived. He looks very apprehensive; he appears a little scared and is clutching his suitcase as if it were a shield that will protect him from whatever is going to happen next. Children in care only ever seem to arrive with one bag, two at the most. I always wondered where all their things were. Mine were in my gran's loft for years.

As I look at his face I am instantly catapulted back to the very situation I had been in. I'm in the social worker's car, just like he is. I have no idea what to expect, what awaits me or even where I am going. My eyes well up as I look at him, and then I quickly push down this unexpected surge of emotion and remember that I am not that child.

I am an adult now, and I make the decision there and then to never look at a young person or child in care as in any way connected to me and my experience. I need to be strong, to try and forget about it.

Besides, I don't really want anyone that I work with to know that I too had a life before this day, that I too have been a child in care, sitting in the car waiting to go to the next home.

Reflection

While I have left the content as it was originally written in my chapters, I have updated the statistics within this chapter. I have reduced the number that I shared originally. In every academic paper, book or web page I have ever read, there are poor outcome statistics, usually as the opening paragraph. These statistics are for policy making rather than for understanding the messiness that is a disrupted and fractured childhood and how we recover from that.

I met Eunice shortly after writing this book, having decided that finding her would be helpful in understanding more about what happened. This led me to access my files, which, as I had suspected, were little more than a catalogue of negative events written through the eyes and perspective of those writing. I'm glad I was in my early 40s before I read them; and yet it is important for the authors of these documents to note that they can be accessed by anyone over 18 years old. Supporting those who write records in files to really understand them as being read by the adult that the child can become has become one of my passions.

Eunice and I have become kind of friends. I say 'kind of' because I feel that Eunice will always remember that she was my social worker first and foremost. It is different for me. For me, Eunice is a colleague, while also being someone who saw me at an incredibly vulnerable time of my life; but, mostly, she is someone I like to have a coffee and a natter with about the state of children's services and the complexity of the cycle of life. She is my friend.

The analogy of the sack of stones really highlights to me the power of writing. Writing this book, meeting Eunice, reading my files, returning to education to do an MA which involved taking the GCSE exams that I had not taken due to school exclusion formed so many of the stones that needed to be removed from the sack. Put the sack down, throw one away. Put the sack down, throw one away.

Discussion Points

How might we ensure that we are involved in sharing many different narratives about the adults that children in care can become?

How will you be remembered by those you are working with now?

What do you carry in your sack of stones that you can throw away?

References

Department for Education (2020a). *Children looked after in England including adoptions*. Retrieved on 8 August 2021 from https://explore-education-statistics.service.gov.uk/find-statistics/children-looked-after-in-england-including-adoptions/2020.

Department for Education (2020b). Outcomes for children looked after by local authorities in England, 31 March 2019. Retrieved on 8 August 2021 from https://assets.publishing.service.gov.uk/government/uploads/system/uploads/attachment_data/file/884758/CLA_Outcomes_Main_Text_2019.pdf.

Sacker, A. et al. (2021). *The lifelong health and wellbeing trajectories of people who have been in care: Findings from the Looked-after Children Grown up Project.* https://mk0nuffieldfounpg9ee.kinstacdn.com/wp-content/uploads/2021/07/The-lifelong-health-and-wellbeing-trajectories-of-people-who-have-been-in-care.pdf.

4
1984–1985

It's February and I'm on the move. So soon. Only six months after arriving at my first foster placement, I am in the car again with one of the many nameless and faceless social workers. I carry many more memories of foster placement number two as I lived with this family for 14 months.

There was a mum, a dad, and one, two, three children all younger than me. A three-bed semi-detached home on a more modern housing estate this time, and the car sitting proudly on this drive had only three wheels. The Robin Reliant appealed to my sense of humour, and the fact that it managed to have all the stability it required with only three wheels instead of the standard four was an interesting symbolism for me to ponder upon.

This was a very different kind of family, but similarly a couple of people working hard to bring up their children, compelled for whatever reason to have an adopted child – the youngest one – and to foster angry, hurting teenagers. In bounces me.

The overwhelming sensation again is one of difference. I can't connect. I am disconnected. Disconnection is a huge part of this experience, and indeed any experience that is painful. By this stage I am disconnected from myself. There is no anchor from which to centre my existence. I have no relationship with my mother, my gran is old and weary and for the life of her doesn't understand what is happening, and my uncle is raising his own family 300 or so miles away. I do not belong anywhere or to anyone; I just come to stay. I can stay a

DOI: 10.4324/9781003257967-7

while in your life and you might care for me for a bit and feed me, but I don't belong here. If I'm truly honest with myself, that sense has never left me, although I have tried to create a deep sense of belonging for my own children, without whom I think I would still be roaming the world, still looking for that beating heart that I belong to. They have taught me all I need to know about love and belonging, but I think I will always carry that particular set of stones in the metaphorical sack that I can pick up and put down whenever I wish.

I've arrived at this placement and they eat pork chops, cabbage and mashed potatoes for their tea (a lot). I have never eaten food like this and it looks horrid and smells disgusting. In the kitchen they also have a hamster endlessly spinning around a wheel in a never-ending marathon of despair. I'd never had a pet in my childhood and I find it strange to see this little ball of brown fluff running around a wheel. So, as my eyes dart round the kitchen, the hamster, the cabbage and the back door to the garden all capture my attention in a flick of an eye, the smell of soggy cabbage lingering long after I've left the room.

The politics of food for children in care has become an ever more fascinating subject for me since I have raised my own children. Food is such a personal thing. I don't think I had ever even seen a pork chop before I entered the second foster placement. Food politics is one of the very interesting things about being a child in care that would bypass most people unless they lived the experience. There is a connection between food and love, and also between food and identity. Food is a cultural thing and a class thing. This is pushed to one side in discussions when we think of children moving between houses and families.

One of the reasons that I cooked up to three meals every evening is that I believed we should eat the foods we like, incorporating a nutritional balance of course! I'm sure that this is a direct result of having no choice about food, what it was, how it was cooked and with the knowledge that it was essentially something that people just 'do', so the differences, the politics of it, are not even considered. If you think about how your emotions and memories are connected to food, you'll probably find a whole heap of assumptions you've taken for granted, alongside some things that you had forgotten.

For example, if you think about your favourite meal, it probably has lots of associations to it. I remember roast chicken on a Sunday cooked by my gran, during the first ten years of my life when I still lived with her. I remember the wish bone that nestled in the breast of the chicken, and of going off into the kitchen under the guise of getting a glass or using some other excuse and then picking chicken off the carcass whilst it was still warm. I try and cook roast chicken every Sunday now and I still pick the chicken off the bone whilst I'm dishing up, and it still makes me feel delightfully naughty. I have no food associations I can recall in relation to my mother. It was my gran who cooked for me; her lovely onions, garlic and olive oil were directly connected to her being French, and she was way ahead of her time in England when it came to food.

Each foster home and each children's home conjures up very different images of different food, and I can tell you vividly about each one. Food is not to be ignored, and yet I never remember anyone discussing food with me.

*

The time came when the lovely foster parents couldn't cope with me any more, and my school couldn't cope with me either because I didn't fit in there. I couldn't bloody cope with me, but I was rather stuck with me! That sensation of isolation, of otherness and of loss of self ran so deep within me that I remember feeling like I couldn't breathe. No amount of external pain would have made any difference to the way I felt. I could have been beaten black and blue and all I would have felt was that I was at least alive. It would not have hurt. I was beyond that. Living with the feeling of not belonging anywhere to anyone was quite enough pain to bear.

The process of not 'fitting in' is twofold: I ensure that I don't fit in through creating an environment in which I can disconnect and I really actually completely don't fit in. If I was ever 'different' before, I have now ensured my place of difference in stone. I am a child in care and I don't know anyone else in my school in the same situation. Well, who the bloody hell am I then? Where is my family? Is my dad looking for me so that he can take me to the place where I 'fit in'? No, because no one is looking for me. Not anybody.

Looking at life in hindsight can be revealing and forgiving, but it can also be oh, so cruel. It is plain to see that no family environment would have been suitable for me. I had never had a father, a relationship that instils the notion of being looked after and having someone there for you who will protect you, a relationship that I have only fathomed in recent years. I didn't even know why there were men; three generations of single women parents and I can be forgiven for this lack of comprehension. I had lived as one of three hurting females, all scrabbling around looking for a protecting force in very different ways. Three generations of single parents with no understanding of their own pain. Alongside that, I had never had siblings, so the concept of sharing time and space with others was always going to be a challenging one. So, again, I had to come to terms with the view that I was different, unable to fit in; that being me was not good, that I was always going to be rejected.

*

I'm in secondary school, perhaps coming towards the end of second year, maybe in third year. It has become quite apparent that my time at the girls' school is not really going to work out. Most lessons are spent in isolation. I have no desire to be a part of this hateful community and I want to die.

Moving from home to home and then school to school taught me many things; but one of the outcomes of all of that movement was the knowledge that if you don't like something, you can change it. It's an interesting lesson as, on the face of it, this is a good thing. It prevents endless moaning about that uncomfortable shift of change,

45

the inevitability of change, the acceptance of change as a part of life. It gives the individual the power to go and do something about things that need changing. From this starting point, everything can be dealt with, changed, removed. What I didn't learn in this place of power, control and wilfulness was that sometimes we have to work through things we don't like. We have to sit in the pain, the discomfort and the growth of not changing, moving or replacing. Sometimes it is by not changing something that the greatest of all changes comes about.

In families people often dislike each other, want time away or struggle with their differences; and mostly, although not exclusively, they learn to forgive and tolerate and work with one another. In 'care' it really doesn't work like that, although again not exclusively, as some children settle into their families so much that they do indeed become one of the family for life.

To explore this further, I want to point out that all parties – and I mean absolutely everyone involved in the life of the child in care – can leave, move on, change the space; and ultimately everyone, except the child, is paid to be there. A social worker can get another job; a foster carer can say that things aren't working out; the school can request a managed move; the child/young person in question can ask to be moved (politely or through enforcing a breakdown of relationships). This is one of the unintended consequences of the system. There are many of these that will be highlighted in the course of this book, and they are very much part of the impact of being in a system where everyone in your life is paid to be there. I believe some of the fallout from being a part of this system of change is an inevitability, and a completely different approach to looking after children who need looking after would be needed to avoid this, one that has yet to be thought of but would perhaps involve a model that had a mix of fostering and that of a children's home with potentially other on-site opportunities in it rather than the 'either/or' approach that we currently have.

*

The new school is a mixed school maybe a mile away from the girls' school, so everyone appears to know me; and my reputation, whatever that was, travels with me in my school satchel. There's nothing 'fresh start' about this new building, and I quickly fall into non-attendance, shouting matches with teachers, exclusions and 'non-engagement'. The breakdown of my second foster family placement coincided neatly with the second school asking me to leave. I think I was excluded, although I can't be certain because the school might have wanted to avoid having the exclusion of a child in care on their records; so it's highly possible that it was called a 'managed move' again.

*

The professionals were running out of ideas and placements. With the breakdown of foster placement number two came the real cherry on the cake of the care experience in Northamptonshire in the 1980s – Tiffield. To some it was a home, for others a holding space. For me this was a terrifying set of three 'units' filled with far angrier and far scarier teenagers than I ever was or had the potential to be. I was housed there for only two weeks but it may as well have been two years. I remember more about those two weeks than I do about places in which I lived for a year.

To try and engage myself in remembering some of the reasons why I was left with the feelings that I had about my two-week stay in Tiffield I decided to conduct some research. I wanted to see if it was still there or whether the building had been sold by the council to become a shopping centre or some other cathedral of despair built on top of the despairing memories held in the very soil upon which it stands – or something else, equally macabre. I also wanted to try and make sense of why it had left such a poignant, bitter taste in my mouth.

During this process, I learnt things that I didn't know back in 1985 as a 15-year-old girl. I found out that in 1996 it became a Secure Unit: a fact that answers many questions for me about the young people I met in there, for, while it was not necessarily a designated named Secure

47

Unit, it was in the middle of nowhere and could only be reached by car, it had a noticeably high staff to young person ratio, and its atmosphere was one of permanent volatility. Even during activities that appeared fairly 'normal', anger could burst out of almost any situation in the most unexpected of ways.

The definition I found for a Secure Unit is 'a residential placement where you are locked up or prevented from leaving'. That is very much how I remember it. It's a little like the sea that looked like a lake. Just because it looks like a lake doesn't mean it is one; if we all know that really it is the sea, why pretend it is a lake? A child placed in a Secure Unit is usually, although not exclusively, awaiting a custodial sentence, at risk of suicide or at risk of harming others.

Prior to being a Secure Unit, Tiffield was also a placement for anyone with nowhere else to go, alongside the self-harmers, the lost children, those awaiting sentencing and the suicide risks; all were likely residents. So you can call it what you like; it was filled with young people with those kinds of needs along with those of us who were simply waiting to find the next placement. I'm sure that there were others like me, others who had arrived in the place accidentally. Are there really any accidents though?

At Tiffield we didn't go to school; schooling was on-site. Education took on a whole new meaning as this was really a classroom of containment. It was one room with desks and books, and all of us were in there together regardless of age. I'm not even certain we went in there every day. We also did sports activities and had the odd singsong with a guy with a guitar.

One of the most interesting things that I have learnt about the human condition during all my experiences is that there is always a pecking order, there is always a hierarchy and there is always someone in charge of determining how that should work best. Divided we fall is more often than not the most likely way of operating. Together we stand only comes into play when there is an opposing force that sits outside your particular sub-group. It matters not where you sit in the societal spectrum as a whole; even if you are all lying on the ground in a heap, there is someone else lying at a slightly elevated level. There is always a hierarchy.

We are all in the gutter, but some of us are looking at the stars.
Oscar Wilde

The way that this plays itself out among clusters of hurting, angry and abandoned young people can be very dangerous when unmanaged by the adults, who themselves may not always have the skills and life experience and support to deal with this well. The hierarchy expresses itself as a complex interweaving of sexual deviance, addictions, violence and offending.

Another discovery I made while researching Tiffield for this book was that there was a history of abuse at the home – not surprising really, given the climate and lack of 'care' given to those 'parented' by the local authority. During the mid- to late-1980s two members of staff were arrested and later charged with sexual offences against girls in Tiffield, including rape and several counts of indecent assault. One of the workers in the home was described in court as a sexual predator, committing sexual offences against girls between 1985 and 1990. His offences were such that he was sentenced to 15 years in prison.

The sex offender, who used the system that was designed to protect children as a place to assault and scar and maim the vulnerable, forgotten children in his care, was working in Tiffield the year I was there. He would take girls out on 'errands' and then rape them in his car in secluded areas. Sometimes he would go into their bedrooms and rape them there.

All of the information I have collected about my time in Tiffield has underpinned the feelings that I had while I was there and why I felt so frightened and vulnerable during my stay. This was an unsafe place to be on so many levels; but I was dropped off there one day and left, once again wondering if someone was going to come and get me soon.

Young people who are in 'care' are vulnerable on so many levels. These children are forgotten children in forgotten buildings. This is why the adult voice of these people has to be heard and given exactly the same amount of value politically as the child's voice – which, even with all the legislation and good practice guidelines in place, is also all too often a silent one.

However, we also have to remember that, for some children, going into care is a saviour compared to the alternative offered by the family home; but the system itself leaves many of its children fighting their way through life at a cost to society that is too high to contemplate. Tiffield Secure Unit was closed down in 2007. May it rest in peace.

The Soundtrack

Material Girl – Madonna
Every Time You Go Away – Paul Young
I Got You Babe – UB40
You Spin Me Round (Like a Record) – Dead Or Alive
Don't You (Forget About Me) – Simple Minds

The Headlines

Live Aid concerts
Brixton riots, sparked by the shooting of Dorothy 'Cherry' Groce
Channel Four launched

The TV

Spitting Image
Eastenders
Happy Days
The Young Ones

Remembered Moments

The Managed Move

It's 2003 and I'm sitting in a meeting with my 'social inclusion' hat on. It's quite an important meeting, filled with head teachers, social workers, social inclusion managers and the like. I am there in the capacity of supporting one of the young people that I am working with who is at risk of being excluded from his secondary school. The discussion is about whether any of the other schools could perhaps take him. This is known as a 'managed move'.

*

It's 1984 and I'm 14 years old, and life at school, in the all-girls' school, is going horribly wrong. There is another school not far away, a mixed school. One of the many meetings held about me with my foster carers, social worker and teacher is about how it might help me to move to this other school.

Being in secondary school was one of the unhappiest times of my life, and that system caused me as much damage as all the other systems that I was engaged in – to me they were all systems of exclusion, of ignorance, of rejection. When I think about school, I think about the word 'exclusion'. Not only because that's invariably what happened to me in the end, but because that's the way I felt.

*

So I'm in the meeting with my work colleagues discussing this boy who we need to keep in the system, and it dawns on me that this discussion had occurred about me: the managed move discussion. I sit there nodding, pondering to myself what it might be like to tell everyone around the table about my managed move, and I chuckle to myself about the irony of it all.

Reflection

That I used to cook three meals each evening so that everyone could have the food they wanted is one of those examples left over from the care experience that I brought into my parenting. I used to feel very pleased with myself for doing this, but it was me that I was healing, not my children. Parenting does that; a parent always wants to do better than they had done to them. Within this intention sits the uniqueness that we bring from our own creation in the moment in time that we were built. Therefore, we are really only ever healing ourselves as we seek to make sure that our children never have to experience some of the things we did – in this instance, eating food in strangers' houses that didn't make any sense. But I was their mum. I was not the stranger. It was our food. I made the food. I could speak of so many examples like this, but just know that this is not about me; this is about how we parent, how we heal and how that manifests whether we are conscious of that process or not. Food helps us feel a sense of belonging.

Belonging runs through all of my chapters in this book, and how it was eroded or cultivated has become of huge interest to me. I am in the process of looking at belonging in my PhD, and I look forward to sharing more about that with everyone in the future.

Finally, the continued background soundtrack to the care experience across many decades has been the abuse that children and young people have endured from a system designed to look after them – looked after largely because they were not able to be properly looked after by anyone else. As mentioned in the Preface, the latest addition to this catalogue of abuse is the report of the Independent Inquiry into Child Sexual Abuse (IICSA), led by Prof. Alexis Jay, regarding Lambeth Council.[1]

Discussion Points

In what ways do you cultivate belonging for those around you?
How was belonging cultivated for you in the different environ-
    ments you spent time in as a child?
What memories come to the fore when you think about certain
    foods?

Note

1 https://www.iicsa.org.uk/publications/investigation/lambeth-council.

5
1986

They have found me somewhere else to go. My two-week externally imposed prison sentence at Tiffield, which I am going to assume was given to me because of a lack of suitable provision elsewhere, was now finally coming to an end.

I can breathe. I no longer need to hold my breath for fear that I will be hurt, or for fear that no one will come and get me. My only hope, Eunice – the social worker with an expanding caseload and a Ford Fiesta – has come to take me away. Here I come, Chalcombe Avenue. After so many moves I actually have no recollection of how long I was here, though a complicated calculation reveals it was probably about nine months.

The home was in a residential area, nestled among all the other houses, integrated into the lives that the TV was showing. Originally two semi-detached houses, they had been knocked together to create a seven- or eight-bedroom house to house us 'lost children', and I spent some time fascinated by the idea that you could enter the building from either front door of what would have been two separate addresses. My memories of this place are of drinking, diversity, complexity and misunderstanding.

The food there was cheap. Back to the food politics; there was no one making any nice home-cooked food here. I remember eating little else but skinny white bread, toasted, soaked in butter, jam and peanut butter. The larder looked like a trader's warehouse, like Costco or a Kwik Save shelf (the Aldi of the 1980s). Endless jars of Happy Shopper

 DOI: 10.4324/9781003257967-8

jam lined the shelves and, because all the food was bought in bulk, the packaging looked different to anything you'd find in a supermarket. I can picture those rows of food so vividly.

This was a 'children's home' in the truest sense. The office was a pokey space the workers would hide and confide in; and, in my imagination, I visualised them all smoking our confiscated cigarettes. When the staff came to work they were in care too; they just didn't realise it. The walls were Institution Cream (aka Magnolia) and lacked anything that made the place a family home. There were no pictures of people having a good time, family groupings, achievements; just empty walls, with the occasional room decorated with incredibly ugly swirly wallpaper.

In this home what stood out was that all of us were completely different. None of us fitted in anywhere; and that, in a strange way, allowed us the opportunity to 'fit in' here. The group of young people in here were a mix and a half. I remember some having learning difficulties; many of us had a cacophony of what could be termed behavioural problems; culturally and racially we spanned at least three continents; and mentally we were all differently disturbed. I now understand that we were all carriers of unresolved, ongoing trauma.

My education had been reduced to a tutor and playing computer games at a Special Unit, somewhere that I cannot recall the name of. By now I was officially being contained. Social Services just needed me to get to 16 to move me on, and to 18 without me killing myself and causing a scandal. I was now associating with some very dangerous people, including a young man who has since spent most of his life in prison – most recently, I believe, for armed robbery to fuel his heroin addiction. (I last heard of his whereabouts – a prison – in about 2002.)

There were also people like me, accidentally in a system we should never have been a part of; but somehow we didn't stick together – we were too caught up in a permanent fight with ourselves, society and everyone around us. We were no support network for one another, and such a thing was never encouraged. Besides, I was destined to live in the tower block that we could see from the window of this 'jam jar home for the alone', with a baby – my keyworker told me so while pointing at it.

*

Although I was unable to articulate it at the time, the two mental states that I learnt to live with during the care experience were **fear** and **survival**.

> **fear**
> *noun*
> a distressing emotion aroused by impending danger, evil, pain, etc., whether the threat is real or imagined; the feeling or condition of being afraid.[1]
>
> **survival**
> *noun*
> the act or fact of surviving, especially under adverse or unusual circumstances.[2]

This was an environment where my risk-taking behaviour could really grab me by the arm and show me places I never want to see again. My drinking was now daily, my self-loathing a natural state; eating rarely took place. This was to be the first of many places that I thought was my rock bottom until I learnt that my emotional pain threshold was so high that I could go far lower than this – and I did, again and again and again.

*

One of the features of families, however strange and dysfunctional they may be, is an element of responsibility. It's a spectrum, of course, but nevertheless there is someone there to pick up the pieces of any mess or disasters made during the formative years. One of the most horrendous aspects of this care system was that when I messed things up, as even the most balanced of teenagers are prone to do (and I was far from balanced), it was down to me. There was no one there. With no support network and a completely broken down relationship with my mother, who was now settled in a new relationship, a grandmother who was in her seventies and an uncle who was focused on raising his own family, I was filled with a complete feeling of aloneness in the truest sense. Since that time I have always considered myself alone, without family and with nowhere to go should I need to.

There was no one to pick up my endless pieces, scattered as they were across the land, highlighting a brightly coloured trail of destruction and devastation.

During the summer of 1986 I was officially allowed to leave school, but by this time I hadn't set foot in a mainstream classroom for nearly two years. My educational experiences were peppered with short spells of home tutoring, on-site 'schooling', work placements and Referral Units. I can almost picture myself staring at a school-leaver's certificate at the grand old age of 16 with an emerging alcohol problem, living in accommodation that was desperate to teach me the skills required for moving on to 'independent living' so I could free up a much-needed bed space, and with no support network whatsoever. How did I get here? How does a little girl with a ponytail and a teddy end up in a place of such self-destruction?

So my time in care was coming to an end and preparations for leaving the final children's home have begun. Prior to the Children Act 1989, I recall these 'preparations' being something of a token gesture. I remember being given my £27 per week allowance and shown how to cook a jacket potato and an omelette. These were, in fact, incredibly helpful skills as living on £27 per week to buy food and pay bills, etc. meant that basically I was a very slender young person. In fact the best way of managing the unmanageable was to forgo eating altogether and concern myself with other more important diet staples such as cigarettes and alcohol. If I had these, then hunger didn't matter. If I had these, then paying the bills didn't matter. If I had these, then my life didn't matter. By the time I was 16 I had learnt the art of self-medication and I could ensure that, in fact, most things didn't need to matter.

Social Services did try and house me, in an independent unit that was supposed to have a member of staff – but I don't remember one being there, ever. There were several of us bright young care leavers though, all nursing our emotional baggage and our inability to communicate. I don't remember being there very long. But I do remember spending most of my pitiful allowance on food and feeling very pleased with myself at my very good budgeting skills, only to have it all stolen by the other residents. I couldn't prove it, but one day I thought I would ask whether my food was being taken, and my room door was forced open. I was punched about the face until the blood covered everything, and that was that. I walked around the streets with my face covered in blood. No one came. No safety for me. I don't know what happened next: a short stay in a YWCA, a move to the Midlands to lodge at a social worker's mum's house. It's all a bit of a blur, but then I ended up in a shared house in Wolverhampton.

In 1986 I came out of care no one's responsibility, with no support, no money and no home. Homelessness really was part of the whole package.

The Soundtrack

Rock Lobster – The B-52s
West End Girls – Pet Shop Boys
Chain Reaction – Diana Ross
Rock Me Amadeus – Falco
Papa Don't Preach – Madonna

The Headlines

John McCarthy is kidnapped in Beirut
Another royal wedding
Chernobyl disaster takes place

First test tube twins are born
Freddie Starr doesn't eat a hamster!

The TV

Miami Vice
The Cosby Show
Dynasty
The Flintstones
Prisoner Cell Block H

Remembered Moments

Who Can Save Me?

I was involved in a 'managed move' from one school to another (excluded), an exclusion from the second school, and my shoplifting habit had taken hold, so I became quite good friends with the Juvenile Liaison Officer, now part of the Youth Offending Team.

There are very few places to go when you hit this particular road of destruction at such a young age. In fact it's a slippery road; it spirals and it goes downhill very fast. It is clear now that each experience placed me one step closer to the next frightening and socially unacceptable place. Everyone could see it, I could feel it, but no one could stop it – my most frightening years.

Reflection

I've long held the view that children coming into care need to be received as in need of a therapeutic intervention, not simply a bed. High-quality relationships, opportunities to discharge toxic stress,

and practitioners who are trauma-informed, working in environments that understand how the legacy of trauma shows up and will alter trajectories across the life course. While we must acknowledge the impact of trauma and understand how this happens in the context of experiences and relationships, we also need to acknowledge and understand our capacity to heal from trauma in the context of experiences and relationships.

The dangerous young man mentioned in this chapter served the final half of his 15-year sentence in Grendon, the only therapeutic prison in the UK. He then went on to spend 18 months in a residential community where he learnt to relate, to work and to live without crime and/or drugs. As I write, he has been living a crime-free life for ten years; and, although there have been many challenges along the way, he has created a life for himself. He is very much a part of my life now, and he inspires me every day.

Discussion Points

When you think of homelessness who or what comes to mind?

Balancing practical needs with emotional support can be challenging. What do you think the priorities should be for young people leaving care?

How can we create a sense of safety for young people coming out of care?

Notes

1 https://www.dictionary.com/browse/fear.
2 https://www.dictionary.com/browse/survival.

6
1987–1989

I really thought I'd seen the worst, that I'd felt the worst I could feel and fallen as low as I could go – and then came the experience of being homeless. An inevitability of being in care in the 1980s was the enforced period of total exclusion from society. I'm sure there were the lucky ones during this time, but this was a world before the Children Act 1989 and the Children (Leaving Care) Act 2000. This was a time when children left care at 16. I was taken shopping with my social worker and we bought cups, cutlery, towels, bed linen and an iron. It was such a fun trip spending all that money, but in real terms, that was it. A few shopping bags of household items, a conversation about buying food and a bed in a shared house that was doomed to fail.

This was not a time of supporting young people through education or hanging on to them until they were 18. This was not a time when knowing the location of the young people in your care was a priority and was measured, with information demanded by the authorities. Times have changed, this is true; but having been in care – even with all the knowledge we have now – is still one of the high-risk factors that leads to homelessness.

*

If I were to associate a word with this experience, it would be detachment – for what else can a person do? It seems to me that removing yourself from yourself, creating an aloofness between you, yourself, the

DOI: 10.4324/9781003257967-9

people around you and the particular experience that you are in, would be a very normal way of dealing with something incomprehensible.

detachment
noun
the act of detaching.
the condition of being detached.[1]

For me to connect with what I was going through would have somehow endorsed it, accepted it, made it ok – and it was far from ok. As I said in the last chapter, I somehow ended up in Wolverhampton. I remember so little about the why and the how of it all, but I know that I was brought to a house; but I have no idea who brought me here or how I ended up in this part of the country. I presume I must have had a social worker somewhere, but I have no recollection of how I came by a social worker in this town. In my memory I don't remember having one outside Northamptonshire, but there we are. Maybe the authorities were alerted that I was still 'in care' when I was looking for accommodation and signing on for benefits so I could feed myself.

The area was called Whitmore Reans and the house looked rather large. I only remember two people from the house. One was a woman that I didn't like at all. She had a child, a seven-year-old boy, and I felt very uncomfortable around her. The other was a boy, a 17-year-old called Pete, and he became my boyfriend for about seven months.

*

After Wolverhampton came Penzance. Again, I have no idea why this even happened, but me and the 'boyfriend of about seven months' got on a train and went to the depths of Cornwall. In the three or four months that I was there I lived in a bed and breakfast, a shared house, a changing cubicle in a disused swimming pool, a train carriage, a tent and a caravan. My most poignant memories of that time were of being homeless in the storms of October 1987 and ending up in hospital with pneumonia, reading *Keep the Aspidistra Flying* by George Orwell, using a launderette to stay warm and being looked at as if I were vermin by the locals.

While the storm was blowing everything into disarray and uprooting cars and trees and flowers and people and dropping them in other places, I had my own internal uprooting going on. Belonging nowhere was now my home. I felt it. I breathed it. I carried it with me everywhere I went. There are two sides to this interesting coin. I can go anywhere and be whoever I want; I am free. Free from obligation, free from expectation, free from who you think I am. Of course the other side of this coin is one of deep aloneness and vulnerability, but I inadvertently chose to take advantage of the former in all its glory.

A huge turning point came for me during the time of *Aspidistra* when I met a journalist from the homeless charity Shelter who was doing a report on homelessness across the country. Even in the mess that was my life, she inspired me. I saw her – I really saw her; I observed her closely: how she spoke, what she wore. I thought about her house and what it might look like and what friends she might have. She was a journalist and she lived in London and I wanted her life.

After my spell in hospital, I got straight on a coach to Victoria in search of this life that I believed I should have. Gazing up at the sky, stunned by the amount of air traffic that London seemed to have, I was blissfully unaware that I had nowhere to go. But London loved me and I loved it back. In the same way that travellers attract other people from their motherland, I attracted other homeless people very quickly who may well have themselves taken the journey and complex route by which one might expect to arrive in London as a homeless teenager. Soon I was also to meet the people who went on to help me. Initially some people I met at the station took me to a squat in King's Cross. Very soon after that, I was introduced to a charity called Alone in London. I quickly became part of the system that protected me and eventually got me off the streets.

I have incredibly vivid memories of my stay at the Centrepoint night shelter, which, back then, was located on Shaftesbury Avenue.

Considering it was a holding space and I was there for less than two weeks, I can picture the staff, the dorms, the people, the feelings – and I can even smell the food. My memories of that fortnight centre on protecting myself from two extremes: the Jesus Army with their gorgeous hot food, and a pimp in a metallic blue Jaguar. Both used young people to 'groom' other young people, with the Jesus Army being slightly more tempting as they lured you into their van with food and hot tea.

The night shelter regime was such that between 8am and 8pm we had to stay outdoors, which left us huddling together in the Trocadero in Piccadilly Circus, begging money from tourists and trying to avoid the seedier side of life. We had luncheon vouchers with which to buy food and drink for the day, but inevitably they were mainly used to purchase cigarettes. At 8pm we would arrive back at the night shelter, where we were greeted with smiles and served amazing food. It was lovely, and such a relief after the coldness of the December air. This faceless love was always welcome.

The rooms were in dorms and the residents were mainly all male. There was the odd woman who stayed in my very own dorm as the 'guests' changed every night, but I was often the only girl. I don't remember ever having any problems with the boys at all; but I remember thinking that some of them were far more vulnerable than I was, and I looked on as the odd boy disappeared into the blue Jaguar with the pimp and I didn't see them again.

From here the system delivered a clear structure, and I was happy for it to do so. Next came the short-stay hostel, then the long-stay shared house, until finally I was found my gorgeous, cockroach-infested, 8th-floor tower block flat on Battersea Park Road where I remained for five years. I lived happily alongside the cockroaches, who were housed in a heating system that gave them the perfect ground for breeding. We didn't meet often but we knew that we were both there, tolerating each other's existences.

In the midst of all this, however, I found the charity Shelter and I plonked myself in their Campaigns Department on the 5th floor. I loved my time at Shelter, but I'm certain I must have been a terrible nuisance! My social skills were poor; I was angry, unstable and desperately lonely. But in the eight months that I was there as a volunteer, they unconditionally loved me without knowing it or probably even meaning to. I worked on Shelter's 21st-anniversary birthday bash, during which I was photographed standing on a podium in Covent Garden with actor Jeremy Irons, gazing up at him in adoration – they used the picture on the front cover of their newspaper. They also paid me £40 to write an article in their magazine, *Roof*. So there I was, a 17-year-old young woman and I am a journalist living in London! Hooray! There was still so much more distance to travel – but this was a little nudge towards me feeling that maybe I was worth something after all.

*

Being housed in the cockroach-infested flat in Battersea in 1988 finally brought to an end two years of homelessness. As well as the nights spent in the B&B, shared house, changing cubicle, train carriage, tent and caravan in Cornwall I'd also slept on people's floors, in a squat, in a bus station, in a launderette, in a hostel, in a bedsit, on a bench and, of course, at the Centrepoint night shelter.

I had been spat on and called names, I'd felt a coldness in my bones I wouldn't wish on anyone, and I had a permanent ache in my belly for food. Every day I was at risk. I was a young woman with an emerging alcohol problem, living in fear of what might happen next. Being homeless is tantamount to being the very scum of society, an experience that still sends me cold when I think about it. These were dark years indeed.

*

There are lots of misconceptions about homelessness and what it actually means. To be vulnerably housed does not mean that someone is necessarily a rough sleeper. To have nowhere safe to go, to feel unsafe where you are, to know that the accommodation you're in is temporary or that you could be thrown out at any time: this is to be homeless.

People become homeless for lots of different reasons. There are social causes of homelessness, such as a lack of affordable housing, poverty and unemployment; and life events which push people into homelessness.

People are forced into homelessness when they leave prison, care or the army with no home to go to. Many women experiencing homelessness have escaped a violent or abusive relationship.

Many people become homeless because they can no longer afford the rent.

And for many, life events like a relationship breaking down, losing a job, mental or physical health problems, or substance misuse put people under considerable strain. Being homeless can, in turn, make many of these problems even harder to resolve. However, in nearly all cases homelessness is preventable and in every case it can be ended.[2]

Since the day that I arrived in my flat on Battersea Park Road, I have never lived in vulnerable housing ever again. I made a very big and real commitment to myself that I would never let that happen to me again and that no one would ever take my home away from me. The feeling of vulnerability when you're homeless – the feeling of having absolutely nowhere to go – cannot really be explained; but I can tell you that living without safety for any period of time changes the very core of you and adds imprints to your soul that will never be removed.

The Soundtrack

It's A Wonderful Life – Black
I Don't Want To Talk About It – Everything But The Girl
Ride On Time – Black Box

Been Around the World – Lisa Stansfield
I Got You Babe – UB40

The Headlines

Terry Waite is kidnapped
Gunman in Hungerford kills 14 people
Thatcher wins an election for the third time
'Black Monday' – the Stock Market crashes
Storms are unpredicted by BBC weather presenter Michael Fish

The TV

No idea …

Remembered Moments

The Phone Box 1987

I'm standing in a phone box in Soho, London. There are adverts all over the tiny square glass windows advertising sexual services. I didn't know I was in Soho or what that actually meant, and I'm not sure I'd ever seen an advert about sex before. I phone my uncle and tell him where I am. I've arrived in London and I'm homeless in London, in a phone box; but I'm ok, I tell him.

Reflection

That my path coincided with a journalist from Shelter, which led me to abruptly make my way to London, strikes me now as a survival strategy that enabled me to move forward at various points and away from the life that I did not want to have. Being able to spot an opportunity and take it is rarely focused upon when thinking about 'building strengths'. This has saved me many times, and I always smile at myself when, yet again, I have been at the intersection of noticing an opportunity and then taking it.

In 2019 Centrepoint celebrated 50 years of working with young people experiencing homelessness, and I was lucky enough to meet up with Nick Hardwick, the charity's CEO at the time that I stayed in its night shelter. It felt poignant because I had been involved in a number of media activities for Centrepoint in the early 1990s, an experience that taught me so much about how to speak about experiences without being used to sell 'abandoned child' fodder for people who are drawn to that. I learnt how to hold myself together and invite people to listen to the back story of political decisions and policy harm rather than get distracted by my own personal story. Unfortunately, those working in charities seeking funding from money pots such as Comic Relief, televised as Friday night entertainment, want the very worst stories as those are what people will give money for. I have been told this a number of times.

While I'm not going to give any kind of analysis about that practice here, it feels prudent to mention that those who share their stories often do so with a personal cost. Everyone in this book has given of themselves generously. It is always important to mention to anyone about to share with you that they own their story and it is up to them what they choose to share with you, as some things are simply private and may remain so forever.

Discussion Points

How do you support people with care experience in sharing their story?

How do you help someone think about their identity so as to help them make sense of themselves?

If you work with young people/adults with care experience, what opportunities do they have to meet others with the same experiences?

Notes

1 https://www.dictionary.com/browse/detachment.
2 https://www.crisis.org.uk/ending-homelessness/about-homelessness/.

7

1990

I have many recollections of drunken stupors. In particular, I remember lying in the middle of the road after drinking almost a bottle of gin, surrounded by people trying to get me up. My recollection of that experience is especially vivid partly because I never touched a drop of gin again. I was 14 years old. Don't blame it on the alcoholic, blame it on the gin! Within that 14-month period of foster home number two, I cemented my addiction to cigarettes, found marijuana and, while I drank slightly less during this period, I knew by now that alcohol was available to me to change the way that I felt – the alcoholic's dream!

*

Once I had left 'care' and was homeless, drinking became a natural way of life. It keeps you warm and it keeps you numb. To sit on the edge of life, of society, of acceptance is not something that one really wants to fully feel. Drink and marijuana dealt with that nicely for me. Self-medicating had been my trusted friend, but it had now become an arch enemy and wanted far more from me than I was prepared to give.

*

My last drink:
    I'm 20 years old. It's Saturday 21st December 1990 and I've gone into the pub at around 5pm for 'a' drink. At this time I've just started studying at college for two A Levels with help from the charity

DOI: 10.4324/9781003257967-10

Buttle UK. I have been housed for two years at this point, so I am living in stable accommodation. I'm quite lost and alone in London really, but I don't care because I'm starting to get somewhere. I'm trying so hard to get my life into some kind of order and so many of the jigsaw pieces are falling into place for this to happen. All but one: alcohol.

I 'come round' at around 3am. I am on my bed in my flat and there are strangers here, and I don't know how I got home or how they got in. I've had a blackout. I'm scared but I can't move. I wake up again at 6am and get up, ready to go to work to start my shift. There is only me here now and I know that I cannot go on or I will die.

*

A blackout experience is one of the worst experiences that alcoholic drinkers have. People have killed during blackouts. It's a complete loss of time in your life. You have no idea what has happened or where you have been. AA meetings are full of people talking about the terror of blackout drinking.

Word in the rooms of AA is that divine intervention supersedes a connection when it comes to Alcoholics Anonymous. I can't argue with that. At 20, I had never heard of AA before, let alone knew how to find them; but sure enough on that Saturday when I returned from work, I picked up the Yellow Pages and phoned them.

A voice asked me for my name and whether I would like anyone to come to my house to talk to me. Absolutely not! But I did learn that there was a meeting at 10pm that very evening, just off the King's Road in Chelsea. That was my first meeting; and that was also my first day sober – and I haven't had a drink since.

AA took the very broken me and pieced me back together, re-wiring me with emotional intelligence, affirmations, self-awareness, self-love and forgiveness – all through a sober looking glass. It was incredibly painful, albeit only slightly less so than continuing the way I was living. It's fair to say that I had no idea that I was even going through all of this for a very long time. But that day in December marked the end and the beginning all at once, and I shall take to the grave the gratitude I feel for the gift of sobriety.

For a number of years life became a daily routine of AA meetings (sometimes up to three a day) alongside university lectures, and endless meetings after the meetings – otherwise known as emotional outpourings and sobriety conversations in coffee shops across London. And while I chose to take the 'bridge to normal living' that AA offered, which means that I haven't been to a meeting for many years, AA gave me a key, a key to my life, for which I will remain grateful forever. Life had begun, finally.

The Soundtrack

> Hotel California – The Eagles
> Wish You Were Here – Pink Floyd
> Groove Is In The Heart – Deee-Lite
> Romeo and Juliet – Dire Straits
> Ride On Time – Black Box

The Headlines

> Poll tax causes demonstrations
> The Berlin Wall is torn down
> Nelson Mandela freed from prison
> Hillsborough claims 96 lives
> Tiananmen Square massacre

The TV

> Still no idea …

Remembered Moments

The Blue Bottle

One of my earliest memories is of drinking a bottle of medicine, a lovely blue bottle of medicine. I've always thought it rather strange that I could recall the colour, but it sat on the edge of my mother's bed in Zetland Street. We shared a bedroom and it had two single beds in it, a little like a hotel room or a dormitory, and the beds had very 1970s' orange eiderdowns on them. This was life before duvets, and it was all sheets and eiderdowns and endless work and skill involved to make the bed. It was a Victorian house and each bed, backed up against the wall, seemed to have its own window to look out of.

There can't have been a security cap on this bottle as I drank the lot. To this day I have no idea what it was or what it was for; but the memory is so vivid as, upon realisation of the bottle's emptiness, I was dragged out of bed while sleeping and thrown over the sink with my gran's fingers down my throat while my mother held me, encouraging me to vomit out the bottle's contents.

As I write this down I sigh a very big sigh. That experience for me was so violent and aggressive yet fuelled by the good intention of keeping me alive and getting the horrid medicine out of me. This poor understanding of me as a real human being, affected by the world around me, dogged the parenting style of both the women who looked after me for those first ten years. Clumsy, thoughtless and over-powering, leaving a large footprint on my memory bank.

Reflection

The attachment to the notion that we are mad, bad or sad pervades most of our services' responses to the use of numbing of pain through addiction. Some people are attracted to the idea that addiction is a

disease or a dis-ease, which comes closer to the reality as to why people choose to do things that numb emotional pain. That the person addicted to shopping is judgemental about the person addicted to heroin is a background noise that supports notions of us and them. But the reality, of course, is that there is no us and them; there are simply humans – humans who have adapted to their environments, within the relationships on offer to them, having the experiences that showed up, while operating with the resources available. Alcohol was available to me and it numbed me.

Without question, the most influential writer on shifting the way we understand trauma, addiction and adaptation is the physician Gabor Maté. He reminds us that healing comes from the word 'whole'. In other words, to heal is 'to become whole'. His seven A's of healing are:

1. Acceptance
2. Awareness
3. Anger
4. Autonomy
5. Attachment
6. Assertion
7. Affirmation (Mate, 2019).

Maté's relentlessness that nudges anyone who will listen to supporting a move away from the medical model towards understanding the legacy of trauma is commendable, alienating and, I imagine, has been at a huge cost to his own wellbeing at times. Putting down my last drink on the 19th December 1990 completely, utterly and dramatically altered the trajectory of my life – and for that I will be forever grateful.

Discussion Points

What judgements do you hold about addiction, and where do these judgements come from?

If you or someone you know needed help with addiction, would you know where to go?

In what way does thinking about the seven A's of healing help your understanding about how we can heal from unresolved pain?

Reference

Maté, G. (2019). *When the Body Says No: The Cost of Hidden Stress*. London: Vermilion.

8
2021

This additional short chapter of mine in the third edition of this book feels essential if for no other reason than it being an opportunity to reflect upon how much we change. Reading back on my writing of 2012/2013 and the sense of detachment from the things that had so deeply troubled me tells me that these originally explored particular layers of the onion have long gone.

I arrive at this point of my life as a menopausal woman with children in their twenties, and studying for a PhD at the University of Oxford. I write down the institution because it makes me smile. That I am doing a PhD at the University of Oxford would have been laughable all those years ago, and now I believe they should be as grateful at having me there as I am at being there. I am more grounded and more complete than I have ever been.

I have been working and living around trauma and recovery for over 30 years now in education and social work settings, and I am continuing to learn and make sense of that space every day. It seems to me that we don't appear to arrive anywhere, yet so much of life seems to be about the illusion of a destination – a place where it all makes sense and, when we get there, all will be well. From where I stand, this is not life at all. It is the journey itself that is the destination and, in that sense, it never ends. Life is full of circles and threads, pulling back together the people we've met, the places we've been and those that came before us and those who come after us. Some people returned to my life only for us to walk away from each other again like

DOI: 10.4324/9781003257967-11

hanging threads that had nowhere left to go in the tapestry that is life, while with others we have formed circles tightly sewn together with loose thread.

Part Two of this book brings generous gifts of many stories, voices, richness and perspectives that I trust will bring you, the reader, more gold. More than that, the authors of the stories have offered reflections on their original writing that provide a real sense of a journey taken, a life lived, a deep reflection of what passed.

Finally, Part Three contains five new chapters that share much about where we have been, where we are now and where we are going. We are rarely at the beginning or the end; rather always somewhere in the middle of a larger story, and Part Three highlights this fluid, connecting aspect of the lived experience of having been in care as a child. I have taken to calling all those who are part of this book the Brightness Family. It feels perfect.

The Soundtrack

Podcasts
Arlo Parks
Dua Lipa
Spotify playlists
Michael Kiwanuka

The Headlines

Covid 19
Travel bans
Black Lives Matter
Trumpism
Harry and Meghan

The TV – What TV?

Netflix
YouTube
Amazon Prime
Reality TV extremes
Sex, Myths and the Menopause

Remembered Moments

I'm staring into my son's eyes. He's about three months old and he has been crying for hours. We are sitting on the bathroom floor, both of us weeping; and, as we have just about exhausted every tear we have, we gaze at one another. I wonder at that moment who gazed at me when I cried as a baby, and then I remember that I will never know. There is no record that exists that can tell me who looked into my eyes for the first few weeks of my life. Then I remember my gran, who would have gazed into my eyes at the first opportunity she was given.

Did my mother? Yes she did. She must have. Because she asked my gran if we could keep the baby …

PART TWO

DOI: 10.4324/9781003257967-12

For each person who contributed their story to this book, I felt drawn to a particular area that I recognised as a part of what we might have dealt with as someone who has been in care either as a child, a young person or an adult.

Every story seemed to have a key element that stood out, and I've defined those elements to associate a single word with each story. In some instances the words I have associated with each person are positive, whereas for others the word is more about the healing process. All the words make sense to me and my story. I wonder if that will be the same for other people who have had similar experiences. Clearly we are never going to experience anything in a one dimensional way, but …

The words I have used for each chapter are:

Education
Recovery
Identity
Connection
Strength
Integrity
Visibility
Literature
Love
Care Activism
Growth
Relationships.

I'm sure the voices you will hear in the next few chapters will also feel an affinity to all of these words through what they have gained, lost and recovered during their experiences. However, you may see and feel different strengths and emotions as you read their stories; but please understand that the words that came to the fore for me are words of recovery and strength, not of pain and weakness.

9
Tim – Education

Tim was taken into care at a very early age. His mother was already in the grip of the mental health service and that gave clear entry for intervention. However, the lack of stability that he was to endure prior to a full care order being taken on him at the age of 12 can't have been easy. Essentially he describes his experience of being in care as one of great success. A loving and stable long-term foster placement, the financial backing supplied under current legislation to support his formal education and his own determination to succeed have meant that Tim has thrived and become the man he wanted to be.

education

noun

1. the act or process of imparting or acquiring general knowledge, developing the powers of reasoning and judgment, and generally of preparing oneself or others intellectually for mature life.
2. the act or process of imparting or acquiring particular knowledge or skills, as for a profession.[1]

*

DOI: 10.4324/9781003257967-13

Tim's Story

I came into care at around three years of age, my wonderful 'life story book' informs me. Unfortunately, my mum had developed mental health issues at a rather young age, and as time went on her condition became worse, to the extent where she felt it extremely difficult to cope and look after her children. My dad barely lived up to his parental responsibilities and I only caught glimpses of him in my life.

My mum and dad split up early on as she, I suppose, realised that he was simply useless, and an awful man. When they separated he never appeared to care, seek contact or contribute anything to the children he had with my mum; there were three of us altogether, and he had two kids with another woman. My mum would have times where she was well and was able to cope; but it was the pregnancies that seemed to trigger her mental health issues, and there would be times where she would have to be sectioned under the Mental Health Act. With no suitable alternative arrangement, all of us children would then have to go into care.

I spent from the age of three up until the age of around 12 going into care, and then back home, into care, and then back home, which must have happened a good 15 times; again, my Life Story Book tells me so. Eventually it became quite apparent that my mother was never going to be able to cope. My mum did battle it out in court; however, she lost her battle, and Leicester City Council subsequently took parental responsibility. Long-term care orders were placed upon her children, and it was not too long after that my brother Rob and I were placed in a long-term foster placement, where we lived for around nine years before heading off to university. We were separated from my other brother, who was given a foster placement elsewhere.

I can honestly say, and I feel forever grateful for this, that when I left care I felt ready to leave. I felt that I had been equipped with the skills to live independently: I had a full-time job, and I was renting accommodation with my brother Rob. This day came, I think, back in April 2011, and that was finally it – I was living on my own two feet. Actually

I feel like I parted from what many would call my 'corporate parents' when I headed off to university, as by this point I had fairly little contact with either my leaving care support and development worker or my foster carers anyway. The leaving care services that I received under S24 of the Children's Act were, I must say, extremely helpful, and I am totally grateful for this support. I did not have to worry about costs associated with the tuition fees, or accommodation; and what's more, I received various grants that assisted me further with the costs associated with going to university.

I always aim to remind people that, without this support, things could have been so very different. I hope that the investment put into me was worth it, and as a result of this investment I would like to think that I will certainly pay all of those costs back. I will be paying my taxes until I retire, as will my children too, because the cycle has been broken.

There are still many care leavers who continue to need society's resources because they didn't have that investment, and sometimes it can be a very difficult cycle to break. Unfortunately there are young people placed into care who do not necessarily get the same deal as I received. I often say that it can sometimes be like a lottery – it's the luck of the draw what deal is handed to you. But I also believe that you're the one that can make that change.

I can only say that, for me, being placed in the care of Leicester City Council has affected me in a positive way, as I feel through being care experienced I have adapted to transition far easier, become that bit more confident than most, and I have developed a mentality which encompasses a 'work hard now, it will pay off later' attitude.

Since becoming a care leaver, I have been employed by a vast number of employers, though I've only changed jobs because of going backwards and forwards from university. I have had no trouble in terms of developing friendships and sustaining those friendships. I have now found my ideal career and I am heading back off to university to study Social Work. I've purchased my first property with my brother, which has gone really well. Never did I think that I would live in a brand new, three-bed detached house with a nice garden and garage, let alone own a house – although I must admit that my late grandmother significantly contributed to making this happen, as she was the one who gave us the deposit we needed.

If I had not been placed into care, I can only think that my life may have turned out a little differently. Perhaps I would not have achieved what I have done; you never know. I am just ecstatic about finding out what life will bring me now.

As I have already alluded to a little, having to mature faster than my non-looked after peers has, without a doubt, propelled me to work hard. Not only that: having to deal with change and transition on so many occasions has made it a far easier process when embarking on my university journeys, moving house and starting new jobs, quite simply because I'm used to it. Going through the care journey, you do come into contact with a vast number of professionals, deal with change, get familiar with the need for procedures and protocols, so you actually learn a fair bit. Another consequence of me experiencing all of this, for me anyway, is that my social skills are strong, as is my confidence and my ability to communicate and voice my opinions to others.

I would highlight independence here. It was clearly very evident when going off to university that my housemates (brilliant guys, by the way) were not as clued up or as streetwise as I was. I can recall taking my housemate food shopping, and he really didn't have much of an idea; he didn't know where things were, or what to buy. Furthermore, when it came to sorting out domestic tasks in the house and dealing with the bills and correspondence, this was something else that I dealt with, as this was what I was used to. This was certainly a strength that I had, which ironically I developed as a result of being 'looked after'.

My housemates came from extremely privileged backgrounds, and for me there was a real sense of achievement to think that I had reached the same level as them. Despite my adverse background, we were at the same university (Leeds), studying the same course (BA Sociology and Social Policy), and we all achieved the same result – a

2:1. (Actually, they both did straight Sociology, so it could be argued that my subject was a little harder because some modules touched on social policy!)

My housemates were aware of my background, and I do feel that I made them think that bit more about people out there in the world who are disadvantaged; and of course I certainly made them appreciate that bit more what they had been dealt in their lives.

Reflection

It is interesting to read what I wrote all those years ago. I maintain the perspective on most of what I shared last time. However, as the years have gone by, I have reflected some more and do not think I would be quite as generous in terms of how I described the care and support provided to me and my brother from our long-term foster carers. I think it can be easy for young people to pretend that all is okay, and some might offer this perspective to protect themselves, as did I, as it can be much easier to heal and recover from adversity when you tell yourself that everything is ok. I will always remain grateful for the care and support I received overall, and I am acutely aware that, without it, I would not be in the position I am in today. Nevertheless, if asked the question now, could my care experiences have been better and or more therapeutic, my response would be, yes – absolutely!

Last time I wrote, I shared my intentions of going back to university to study social work. Having already acquired a bachelor's degree and a master's, I had hoped this would not have posed too many challenges; but how wrong was I. I studied on two different social work courses, and on both occasions I encountered some big issues which prevented me from qualifying as a social worker. I must be the most qualified social worker in the land without the social work qualification. I needed to draw on my resilience in overcoming these challenges, and it really was tough. I was quite shocked by some of the practices I observed, which at times were certainly not supportive; rather, quite oppressive, which is the last thing I ever would have expected when studying on a social work course.

I had to move on and quickly found another position. I began working for a Local Authority Virtual School as an Education Improvement Officer, and worked other posts alongside as this role was only part time. I was so happy but also very relieved. I had also managed to appear on a TV gameshow, a sibling special *Deal or No Deal*. This could not have come at a better time, as I took part only a day after exiting my social work course at the second attempt. My brother and I did well on the show and banked a good amount of cash and won a holiday to Thailand, so this certainly gave me a lift! I did find myself thinking, what next? ... Do I go and enrol for a third time? But instead I turned my attention to an alternative career and felt I could offer a lot more in this area. I worked in children's homes, and felt this was the career for me. However I quickly became disillusioned in the homes I worked at, and felt I could do better and offer a better home environment with the right care and support. With a touch of good fortune, along with sheer hard work, I managed to set up my own residential children's home company, called T-Junction Children's Services. We have been operating now since 2017, and we continue to go from strength to strength. However the industry is, without a doubt, hard going, in the sense that one day everything can be fine and the next day you can find yourself in a really bad place, managing all manner of situations which can also see children's homes being closed down quite promptly. We have two homes, and are due to open our third home shortly; and I have to say that I absolutely love the work I do.

I relish sharing my experiences in the hope this will bring about change and improvements to services and outcomes for children in care. It does genuinely upset me when I read about companies that own and provide residential services and yet have never even worked in homes – and, in some cases, not worked with children in care. There has been lots of material in the media about the profiteering of companies in the sector, and poor outcomes being achieved and or poor services being provided. Equally, lots of providers sharing they offer therapeutic care, which is just not the case. These are the people I would love to meet and work with, and feel my contributions could be much needed.

One day I would also like to follow in Lisa's footsteps and write a book, and would relish sharing experiences in my life that might broaden people's awareness of issues impacting on children in care, and also that pays attention to what it takes to make the difference and be the best corporate parent you can in supporting children in care with their recovery. My experiences have also taught me that drawing on resilience is just as important now (in adulthood) as it was when growing up in care.

On a personal note, I married two years ago and my wife Alex and I are expecting our first child this November (2021). We are both very excited. We also moved into our family home just over a year ago, and each day I count my blessings and pinch myself as I can't believe how I managed to get myself to this position. That said, I also have lots of worries and insecurities about returning to a life of adversity and things in life failing. I think this also partly explains why I am so keen to diversify the work I do, so if one did fail I can keep going with another and sustain the life I currently live. I do sometimes find myself reflecting on how different my life could have been, and sometimes think about some of the really bad times and poor experiences I had to endure, where there is no doubt in my mind that I overcame some serious odds in getting myself to where I am today.

I am also forever grateful for the support and legacy my grandparents left behind. Without their support and leg-up, there is no doubt that my life would have been more of a struggle and it would have been more difficult to get to where I am today. That said, I had to endure several misfortunes and unfortunate events to be in this position, so this has always felt bittersweet.

Discussion Points

Does Tim's reflection that he would be less generous about his experiences now than he was when he first wrote his chapter surprise you?

Whether yes or no, why?

What do you think Tim means when he says that his experience could have been more therapeutic?

Note

1 https://www.dictionary.com/browse/education.

10

Jane – Recovery

I was introduced to Jane by a close friend. He knew bits of her story and thought she would be a good person for the book. Jane's story blew me away. Her own journey into care was harrowing enough without the late 1960s' and 1970s' approach to children in need of 'care'.

recovery
noun

1. an act of recovering.
2. the regaining of or possibility of regaining something lost or taken away.
3. restoration or return to health from sickness.
4. restoration or return to any former and better state or condition.[1]

Jane is 50 years old and has a story that is harrowing and unbelievable in equal measure; yet this successful woman sits before me, kindly offering to share that which has been unspoken for a long time.

*

DOI: 10.4324/9781003257967-14

Jane's Story

As far as social services and the police were concerned, the reason that my sister and my brother and I were taken into care was because we didn't attend school for a year. We were homeless, which meant that we moved about an awful lot. We also had no money because we were homeless, and my mother couldn't get any support because we were outside of the system; so, to bring in money, she became a sex worker.

We moved about constantly and lived an unbelievably dangerous lifestyle because of some of the places that we ended up staying in. Some of the men's homes we stayed in my sister and I were abused by these men. So yes it was quite horrifically dangerous; we were incredibly vulnerable and in desperate need of protection.

The background to us being homeless and not attending school for a year was quite horrific. I'd had a childhood full of abuse of all kinds. I was sexually abused by numerous abusers, one of whom was my eldest brother. That had happened from, I would guess, about the age of seven years old; but I don't really know.

My mother and father were never married, which was unusual in those days, but we were his second family. There were five of us children and he abandoned us when I was just ten years old. We survived for a while because he was still supporting us financially as a family. Then my eldest brother, who was my abuser, got hit by a car and died when he was 17. I was then 12 and had just started high school.

Not long after my brother died, my mother sent us with a few belongings to a male friend of hers, with a note for him to look after us, and she attempted suicide that night. So she was hospitalised and we were farmed out by my father to different members of our extended family. My dad was back on the scene again for a short time. While we were staying with these family members and Mum was in a psychiatric hospital receiving electric shock treatment, my dad sold our family home, had a huge bonfire and destroyed all our belongings.

She could do nothing even when she was well enough, because they weren't married.

So, she came out of hospital and we were homeless – we had nothing and nowhere to go. We stayed with the same male friend of hers for a while in an overcrowded council house. This was the year we were homeless, moving around, being abused. I remember phoning for ambulances as my mother was physically beaten regularly by her boyfriend/pimp. He was also one of my sexual abusers. He went on years later to murder a man in a row over the price of a can of soft drink. At last he was sent to prison.

I arrived into care and the one thing I remember was feeling safe. At last I was safe. My sister and I felt that really strongly; it was safe and she wasn't around. The dreadful thing about it was that we were separated from my brother who was six years younger than me, so he was six years old – just a child.

In those days, if you were in care long term it was separate children's homes – in Walsall there was a home for boys and a home for girls. The impact of that decision is that I don't really know him. My sister and I are very close – she left for London when she was 16; she ran away. So she has less of a relationship with my brother than I do and I don't have a good relationship with him. I don't know him.

Even though we felt safe, I have abiding memories of a loveless environment. I vividly remember the regimentation, the type of institutional obsessions with certain elements of everyday life which helps the institution run more smoothly for staff, but is not child-centred! For example, we had a very early wake-up (around 6.30, which was when morning staff came on duty), followed by a strict rule about getting up, using the bathroom, making beds and being downstairs in 20 minutes. The older children had to make the beds of younger girls; we had one or two each depending on the makeup of the ages of those in the home at any one time.

The beds would be inspected and torn apart if not up to scratch. All very much about power and control, reinforcement by the matron! I remember the younger child whose bed I had to make used to wet her bed, and we tried to sneak this past the matron; but this was very difficult because there were areas where anything was stored that were out of bounds (the implication was we were all thieves so permission was needed for everything).

Inevitably this child, Sharon (of about five years old), would be found out and she had to, for her punishment, hand-wash her sheets in a bucket in the utilities area while the rest of us had breakfast. The humiliation and damage done by this cruelty we can only guess at. I learnt recently, two years ago in fact, that she had been a 'battered' woman all her life and was eventually murdered by her partner two years ago.

The 'little uns', as we called them, were lovely. I felt so sad for them. We tried to cheer them up as best we could. The matron had her favourites, and she was quite open and obvious about it. They received preferential treatment and the rest of us looked on powerless. I believe that my feelings about fighting all injustice and racism began then. I've been told, because I don't remember, that when they all had chickenpox I read stories to them. I believe I probably did because I was always reading to myself and others. I see the teacher in me even then!

Every Christmas and Easter we had presents from local women who worked in local shops and factories, strangers who we never met. At first I didn't understand why we were seen as 'charity cases'. I had never viewed myself from that perspective. But I understood it for the younger ones, who I realised, some of them, had no one outside. I never forgot their kindness, and although they were anonymous they wrote our names on each gift card as if they knew us. It's meant that as an adult I have fostered difficult teens and supported children through organisations like Plan International, and worked as a volunteer for various charities like Stepping Stones and Samaritans. I'll never forget 'from all the girls at Littlewoods' and 'all the girls at Crabtrees', and the thought that someone cared who didn't even know us.

The court order was rescinded when we got to the age of 15 for my sister and 16 for me. I understand this to be because we had been taken into care due to non-attendance of school, so as soon as the legal school leaving age was reached we were sent back home. Of course, the abuse started again straight away, for both of us. And this time it was the same boyfriend who had abused me who was now abusing my sister.

Having been in care meant that, when I went back home, I knew that things had to be different, and after many rows I was beaten and thrown out of the house. My sister ran away a few days later and she never came back.

We were still so very vulnerable and I had been targeted while I was in care by a man who was six years older than me. Very quickly I was pregnant. I think that I was looking for affection. Care is a *loveless* place: there is *no* love whatsoever in there; we didn't see it and we didn't find it. All we saw was more abuse. It was a different kind of abuse, but abuse all the same.

So I was pregnant and in a very abusive relationship, which unfortunately I have to say lasted 19 years. So for a further 19 years I was abused. I had low self-esteem and everything that goes with that, and it took me that long to be able to work on myself and get myself together so that I was strong enough to leave. Which I knew would be dangerously *horrific*, and it was. But I was determined to leave – I wasn't taking it any more. I remember thinking: 'Is this my life, is this it, is this all there is?'

What might have helped me and put the brakes on my living out the next 19 years in fear would have been when I was first at home with my young children. I was determined to achieve my ambition to be a teacher, and when they were toddlers I started going to the local FE college one evening a week to evening classes to gain my A Levels. That took two years, and then I started teaching a bit of ESOL in a home tutoring, voluntary scheme. As soon as they were both at school full time, aged 5 and 6 years old, I got a place at a local university and studied for a degree and a teaching qualification. *That* would have been the time, because that was my real time of growth. But life took over with working, raising my children and managing the abusive relationship.

Education was the key for me. I loved it and I absolutely thrived on it, and that is one thing I took into adulthood. I *love* learning and to go into teaching was just a natural thing for me, to pass on that love of learning and to help and empower others. I just love it. If anyone could have helped me with my personal development that would have been the time I think.

When I think about what I have gained from all of those experiences I think one of things about me is that I am resilient: no matter how many times I get knocked down, I get back up again. I don't think it's possible to get to where I am now without it, and that's one of the things about me that I am most proud of. That is not to say that there haven't been times when I have wanted to end it all, because there have. Depression has presented itself a couple of times. I often feel like an outsider in groups of people. My experience separates me, but also connects me with others who have had similar experiences. I think we recognise something in each other. We've got through it all and come out the other side. I'm definitely a survivor.

Reflection

Immediately, following the interview, I naturally focused on the trauma of that time. When we recount our stories they live once again in our psyche; for a short time they are quite raw again. So, the feelings of lovelessness, fear and loneliness returned. In addition, however, something changed dramatically. I began to think differently about my time in care: that it was worth something, it had a value, and it was an experience worth telling. I know this sounds strange, but I had always viewed that time in my life as rather a secret, or not of great interest to anyone. I did not talk about it with people mainly because it's difficult for the non-care experienced to understand ... Previously, if mentioned the first question I would be asked was "What did you do to end up in care?" NOT "What happened to you?" Why would I want to answer that kind of question?

I think that it was also kept hidden because it was a time of low self-esteem and invisibility. Institutions do that: the unkindness, the routines and the efficient systems of the care home generate feelings that you don't matter. In talking about it to someone who was interested and understood, I began to value my lived experience of care; it's what separates me, but also what brings me closer to others from a similar experience, and even gives me a sense of belonging.

In an attempt to process the feelings and thoughts brought to the fore once again, I researched the area of childhood trauma and resilience and came across the theory of ACEs, or Adverse Childhood Experiences, and the effects on care experienced children in particular. I recognise that I experienced all ten adverse childhood experiences. I believe, more strongly than ever, that education was my escape, my way out, my salvation. My life path could have been much more difficult and dangerous. I recalled later one person who made me feel cared about at school. She was the Senior Mistress, responsible for the behaviour of the girls, and numerous times I would be ordered out of the classroom because I was wearing mascara. She would send me to the girls' toilets to wash it off. I never did, but she would join me 10 minutes later and ask me how I was and how my sister and I were coping. It only took one teacher to show she cared, and I excelled in all my subjects. I gained more A*s than anyone ever had previously at that school!

Since the interview I changed career and my newfound knowledge and passion has led me to work as a Deputy Head in a virtual school. Virtual schools work for children in care to have the best education possible, and they liaise between social workers and children and school heads. My experiences, at last, are being used in a positive way. I am able to fight for children in care to have the best possible opportunity to succeed. Children in care need to have access to at least one person of trust to form a trusted relationship. They also need the effects of trauma they have and are experiencing to be addressed.

In reflecting on the piece now, I feel that I was so fortunate to have a person who I trusted and who cared about me at school. I survived it all and had the courage to heal. As a child I had no choice; I was a victim of abuse, a victim of the care system and a victim of a bully as a teenager and young mother. However, having the courage to heal, I resigned myself to choose to no longer be a victim. Through education, self-care and self-development, I was able to choose who I was and am today. I count myself as one of the lucky ones.

Discussion Points

The experience of safeguarding and of being in care that Jane describes makes for a harrowing read. Were you shocked by it?

Why did you answer in that way?

Jane describes herself as one of the lucky ones. What thoughts and feelings does that bring up in you?

Note

1 https://www.dictionary.com/browse/recovery.

11
Noel – Identity

There is so much research around identity and the difference that is made when our identities are handled well that it begs the question why it still has to be highlighted as an area in need of further understanding – but it does. The discussions remain about improvements that need to be made to policies and procedures around adoption.

identity
noun

1. the state or fact of remaining the same one or ones, as under varying aspects or conditions: *The identity of the fingerprints on the gun with those on file provided evidence that he was the killer.*
2. the condition of being oneself or itself, and not another: *He began to doubt his own identity.*
3. condition or character as to who a person or what a thing is; the qualities, beliefs, etc., that distinguish or identify a person or thing: *a case of mistaken identity; a male gender identity; immigrants with strong ethnic identities.*[1]

Feeling excluded will only ever ensure negative outcomes for children and young people as they develop and move through the transition into adulthood. The sense of not belonging to a group, a family, a school, an area alongside the differences experienced while being 'looked after' can cause a number of responses. A child or young person may choose to self-exclude as a means of protection, retreat into 'another world', seek out others with the same issues and form meaningful but often damaging alliances, or learn to self-medicate on drugs and alcohol, for example, rather than live with the sensation of isolation or even feel suicidal.

While this is going on at a level that is more easily accessible, the issues around identity regarding culture, religion and unidentified parents, for example, create a much deeper feeling of an unknown identity. Put these two places of unresolved states together and throw in some developmental confusion and general teenage angst as well and we have a very lost and hurt child/young person.

Noel found me on one of the Facebook groups that I am in after I started talking about this book. He sent me a message saying that he might be able to help me as he had been adopted. We arranged to meet in a pub in Chipping Norton and I asked him how I might be able to spot him. He replied, "Don't worry. I'll be the only man in the bar with dreadlocks. You won't miss me." Now if you've ever been to Chipping Norton in the Cotswolds, you'll appreciate how amusing a thought that is: it is the land of Middle England, the Hunt, golf and horse riding, and where the *Daily Mail* is the paper of choice in most establishments. Much of Oxfordshire, the county I currently find myself living in, could be described in this way without looking too deeply. So, as he had suggested, Noel was indeed incredibly easy to spot.

*

Noel's Story

Trying to piece together what happened and where I have come from has been tricky; it's a long time ago. I saw the court reports to do with my adoption and, reading in between the lines, my birth mother was in a bad place. She gave birth to me and stayed in hospital for however long she had to, which in those days I'm guessing was about four or five days. She developed a pattern of leaving me there and coming back a number of times over a period of about two or three months, each time saying that she was going to take me home. Each time, she kept leaving me. In the end she just upped and left and never came back. She left me there for the authorities to deal with. And that's how I came to be in care with foster parents until subsequently I was adopted.

Again, looking at court reports – because obviously I was too young to remember – there was a lot of to-ing and fro-ing going on; but, from what I can gather, *happy* to-ing and fro-ing. The court reports themselves make no mention of me being an unhappy child; I am always referred to as a *happy* child and one that someone would be quite happy to have. I would conclude from that that during those three and a half years where I was 'passed from pillar to post' I was actually *happy*. I think I was shown quite a lot of lightness and love. I am a happy person. I wake up every morning always thinking positively, thinking that something good is going to happen today, and I think that is the best way to live your life. I think if you start off negative you tend to bring the world down around you, so I've always been happy. It's not an act; I don't go home, close the curtains and cry! I try to find the good in everyone.

I met my mum when I was 15 years old. It really didn't help me in any way, and in fact just brought more confusion. When I had read the reports about my adoption there were lots of mentions of siblings, and siblings being adopted out as well – and I'm actually a twin! He was adopted out too and I met him at that first meeting with my birth mother but I completely disregarded him. He was there because he was welcomed back into the family and I wasn't, and I was a bit unprepared for that. Because I was 15 and dealing with my own 'stuff' as a teenager, trying to make sense of everything, I hadn't really prepared myself or done enough research. I was in too much of a rush; it was a very impulsive thing I did. But subsequently I have been back since around the time I was aged 29/30, and that was a lot better as I was more prepared. I also sat down and talked to my brother and I have talked to my mother *better*, although I still haven't quite got the answers. I very much doubt I'll ever see them again, but I got quite a lot more resolved because I was a lot older.

It was around 1991 when I made that first visit to my birth mother. As an adoptee trying to find the people that gave birth to you, the avenues that were available to me were absolute rubbish. I really cannot see the point of withholding somebody's birth certificate; I really can't see the logic in that at all. I think anyone that gives someone up for adoption must always realise that at some point that person might come knocking on your door; it's just human nature, so why the government and everyone else turn their back on the poor person who never *chose* to be adopted out in the first place is beyond me. I had nowhere to turn to get help, and no one seemed to know who exactly could help me. I think now that access to documents has got better. You can now get your original birth certificate and that's not an issue; but I still don't think there is enough support there. No one helped me at all during that time and no one was remotely interested in what I needed to do, and I'm not sure how much that has changed.

I must add at this point that I was very very lucky. The parents that adopted me were very organised, a 'belt and braces' family. They kept the driving licences in a box in the sideboard, and they kept all my adoptive papers. I consider this to be a very lucky thing for me because had they not I would never have seen them. However, as I had no one helping me manage my need to meet my birth parents, I don't think anyone was helping my adoptive family either.

My mum was a teacher and my father was a youth worker. They were white and I am black. The whole interracial adoption was a lot easier back then and, as a teacher and a youth worker, I don't think you could have picked two better professions. I think the courts just stamped the papers. I think the court just said absolutely, you've already got a daughter yourselves, you're obviously good with children, and away you go. I'm not certain that anyone ever sat down with them and said, do you know what? You love this child, you put plaster on his knees, you feed him, you clothe him, you cuddle him when he's upset. You do realise that at some point he might turn his back on you and try and find his birth mother? I don't think anyone ever told them that. So when I did need to meet my birth mother it seriously affected my relationship with them.

We are over it now, but it caused a massive rift for years. Looking back, we always thought it was something else, but that's where it stems from – this desire for me to go and see my mum – and they didn't stop me, they applauded it; they said you should do and here's all your paperwork. But they didn't know how to deal with it. I didn't know how to deal with it either and, more importantly, there was no one there to help us or tell us how to put the pieces back together afterwards. And I can see that when you bring someone up for 15 years, treat them as your own, give them everything they could possibly want and they say sorry, I'm off to find the person who gave birth to me, it must be so cruel. Of course at 15 I didn't know it had an impact on them. I wonder if the support network is there now. It was only a year or so after that I moved out of home and things were never quite the same again, although we did recover to a large degree, but that took about eight or nine years.

During that time I never talked about all the things that were happening because I could never put my finger on that being the trigger and the catalyst for it. I didn't understand it all myself.

I have no idea about my dad and I haven't really delved into it too much. For me it is an unresolved issue. Is it because I want to know who he is? Is it because I want to make myself complete? Or is it purely just because it bugs me? I don't know. I wonder how much of me does actually want to meet my father. I would guess that actually, in a funny way, very little of me really does want to meet him. In the same vein *all of me wants to meet him*.

The best way I can explain it is to differentiate between want and need. Do I want to meet him? Do I need to see him? Do I *want* to see him? No, not particularly. I've lived quite happily for 36 years and

I'll live the rest of my life happily without seeing him. Do I *need* to see him? Probably yes, because there will always be that element of doubt and upset. So yes, want and need are probably the best way to describe this conundrum. My mother was very tight-lipped and wouldn't say anything about him, and his name isn't on the birth certificate; so, unless she actually divulges who he was, I shall have to go to the grave not knowing.

I think everyone will always want to know where they came from; who their mother and father were, under what circumstances they were born etc., and I think everyone would feel that they have that gap in their life if they didn't know. I've *still* got that gap in my life and, yes, it is going to leave some questions unanswered, which is inevitable unfortunately.

The main thing that stems from the *psychology* of being adopted is around not necessarily being wanted and of being on your own, which has always led me to be an individual and therefore just to go and explore the world. A lot of people like the safety blanket; they would never just get on a plane and go and live in Italy for three months or just go and put all their life savings on red on a roulette wheel. So as an adult I suppose I do gamble with life sometimes, because there has never been anyone there to say look, this is the right thing to do or this is the wrong thing to do; there were never any boundaries set.

By being given up for adoption and because of that lack of boundaries, I find myself wandering off. I am known for being a bit of a traveller and a wanderer – have passport, will travel! I believe that for me, that this stems from my adoption, because I lived without those boundaries.

The good side of that is that I look back at my passport and it's got some incredible stamps from all around the world, nearly every continent, some incredible parties and amazing people, some fantastic times and incredible memories and opportunities – things that people will never get to do. The sad side to all that is that I never quite finish anything though. My CV is full of one job after another because I could never just stay there, because there were never the boundaries.

So that's the one major thing that has affected me from being adopted, and that's boundaries.

I don't feel unique, but some of the scenarios I come up against feel unique to me. When I've taken long-haul journeys and I'm asked questions about my family medical history, of course I don't have a clue. I have absolutely no idea about my medical history. When I went on holiday to Jamaica, where I know my mum came from, I spent half the holiday thinking perhaps my nan lives in that house!

The biggest outcome from having lived the life I have is that I put up barriers. I absolutely believe that I put up barriers because – and it's a total cliché – I was abandoned by the person who was supposed to love me more than anyone else, and it is because of these barriers that I think friends have suffered. Partners have definitely suffered and it's not their fault, but I won't open up to them. I just will not open up because of that fear of rejection, and I carry that around with me everywhere I go, which is a terrible shame, and I'm sure that it stems from adoption.

Reflection

I look back at my life at times when I have the time to think. It's been sad, funny complicated and a list of emotions that would fill this page. Sometimes I think it isn't any different to anyone else's, and sometimes I think it's special.

I don't regret anything in my life and try and live it to the full every day. I've noticed I have a propensity to try and help everyone around me, which often makes me think am I trying to hide my own sadness or am I just trying to be a better person?

There is a deep-rooted sadness inside, largely because of the loss of life and a fragmented family history. I often wonder if being part of my biological family would have helped change this. However I also realise you can't look back in anger; you have to take what life throws at you and keep moving forward.

Most importantly now at mid-life I hold no grudges against family that left me and also accept that, like someone who is homeless, I'll keep going from one situation to another trying to help those that struggle until I find a place called home.

As life stands now I realise I do have family – they are work colleagues, surrogate nieces and nephews, next-door neighbours and alike – and, as I cherish these, I know I'll be okay and keep fighting every day to find home.

Discussion Points

What do you think of when you think of 'home'?

In what ways has the adoption process altered now?

Do you think all those with disrupted childhoods will eventually seek answers to where they come from?

Note

1 https://www.dictionary.com/browse/identity.

12
Dianne – Connection

Dianne found me on Twitter. I love Twitter so much and have made some amazing acquaintances and friends using this medium.

For me, Dianne is all about connection: connection to self.

connection
noun

1. the act or state of connecting; union
2. something that connects, joins, or relates; link or bond
3. a relationship or association.[1]

*

Dianne's Story

Ironically, feeling like a 'nobody' as a child has helped me develop a strong sense of 'me'. I knew that whoever I was or wasn't, I was 'Dianne'. Whilst I didn't value her or believe that anyone else did, she was the only person on the planet on whom I could rely. Not in a big, loud, in-your-face way but in a cool, calm, quiet way. As a teenager I was a real loner, spending most of those years alone both at home and at school. I developed the ability to be both physically present but emotionally absent at the same time. Protecting the gentle soul within.

DOI: 10.4324/9781003257967-16

Whilst spending all my childhood trying to please the adults around me in order to fit in and receive their love, I developed a strong sense of right and wrong. I needed to discover what was going to give me a smile and good attention rather than being ignored or worse. The positive side of being 'good' all the time was it saved me from sliding into the darker side of life.

I had several opportunities as an attractive young woman to take seemingly easier options to gain a comfortable lifestyle and receive 'love'. However, I appeared to have developed a strong moral sense: I knew where the line was and I wasn't prepared to cross it.

Whilst this was a fear-based mindset I am sure ultimately it saved my life and, more importantly, maintained my integrity. This has stayed with me all my life. It is a strange dichotomy that, whilst I didn't value who I was, I knew that I had to keep safe all that I was.

I am grateful for that, and I believe it is a direct result of my experiences as an unloved child.

I cannot count the times that people have said to me: "I can't believe you were in care, you seem so … normal/well balanced." There is a perception that children in care come from backgrounds that are of a type. And those children will always emerge damaged from their homes and the system. For me the experiences of those years were indeed profoundly negative.

However, they were also a fertile ground for encouraging me to seek out the valuable, lovable me. Yes, there has been, and is, a lot of introspection; however, I have learnt to love myself as I am loved by the many others in my life. My life has unfurled, petal by petal, revealing that gentle precious soul that had retreated to avoid decimation by the so-called carers around her.

I have a complete lack of bitterness about my experiences; I have come to accept that the key players all had their own 'stuff' going on. However, losing my mother at two years of age meant I lost the person who truly cherished me, the way I cherish my children. That loss was accompanied by indifference or neglect.

This has also allowed me to have an unerring ability to see both sides of any and every situation. I don't judge; I accept that everyone operates with what they have.

The biggest lesson I learnt from all of this was that I have a choice. I can choose to hate the people who caused me so much pain, turned their back on me and ignored my needs. I could have chosen to medicate myself through those years with one substance or another. I could have taken up some of the very dodgy offers of 'help' I was given. I could have chosen to turn my back on my values and do whatever I had to do to run with the crowd, any crowd. Instead, for the most part, I chose to observe and learn from everything and everyone.

I confess I didn't consciously decide I wasn't going to be defined by my experiences as a child until after I was married. Up until that time I realise now that I was doing that innately. When my children were born, however, I realised that I was looking through a filter of fear at every aspect of life and my strategy was to disengage when the going got tough.

I spent my childhood with people who had 'disengaged' from me. I wasn't going to do that with my precious babies. So I made different choices, every step of the way, re-engaging me with all the emotions I had been suppressing to survive. It was painful – but worth it.

I was a timid, unadventurous child and young person, never ever stepping outside my immediate comfort zone in any situation. However, ultimately my experiences have allowed me to live my life back to front. The freedom and love I didn't have as a child, I have now.

I am interminably inquisitive! Constantly curious, peering into new subjects, learning new skills and expanding my knowledge. The fear that kept me safe and confined in a controlled emotional environment has been a springboard to explore and engage in new experiences. I truly believe that life gets better, not worse.

Those formative years on my own without guidance and support have meant that eventually, with age, I have developed the growing confidence in myself and in my ability to make good decisions.

Now in my fifties, I am free to be me! Warts and all! I am more outspoken than ever before and not necessarily the 'pussy cat' I was, which inevitably brings different problems.

However, that's okay because finally Dianne has found her voice, and she likes the sound of it!

Reflection

It's illuminating rereading my words of ten years ago. How 'together' I sounded. How sorted. There wasn't much comment on the amount of therapy I'd had to get me to that apparent place of peace. At the time I thought, for the most part, I had arrived. Ah, how naïve. The confidence I'd gained over the years from a stable marriage led me to believe my childhood wounds were healed. The scars had faded and any residual impact neatly neutralised by clever words from equally clever therapists. However, I've learnt that this is far from the truth. The passage from my fifties to sixties brought new painful insights. Most of this realisation came about through the birth of my two grandsons in the last three years.

Even though I'm as busy as a grandmother as I was as a mother, I seem to have more time to observe and appreciate the little ones. With the day-to-day care the responsibility of their mothers, I am free to notice every mood, every whim and every new thing they do. One of them lives with me along with his parents. I have experienced him from a bump to now a toddler. It has been a unique, beautiful and challenging experience. His moods now, like all toddlers, are epic; everything is either wonderful or dreadful. What was fun one day is torture the next. He lets us believe we've got it sorted with a workable routine until he decides otherwise. It is his world. His parents and I make room for all this and work with it. He will no doubt grow up feeling loved, valued, special, and absolutely owning his part of the universe. His experience of the world as a toddler could not be more different than mine. Observing the care, love and understanding he receives has acted as catalyst to crack open the façade of acceptance of my history. Currently he is two years and eight months old; exactly the age I was when my mother died suddenly.

Unfortunately, proximity to my grandson has had an unexpectedly deeply unsettling effect. I can no longer pretend I'm alright with my past. After all this time I can say it hurts deeply to reflect on my early years. His presence has opened a fissure in a boiling volcano of injustice and hate for my caregivers that I can't hide from any more. I have come to realise that, whilst I survived a painful childhood, I am more wounded than I thought. When I wrote about my time in care ten years ago, I did acknowledge that disengaging was my primary superpower for survival. Whilst there have been true benefits from being able to detach from emotional pain, there is also an unbidden numbness that's shrouded the good stuff too. I'd clearly strategised my way through life. Being a deep thinker mostly saved me from the worst effects of neglect as I used intellectualising as a defence in understanding the actions of those around me. Those painful experiences which started brutally as a toddler didn't just damage my emotional being; they amputated great chunks of it. Equally, with this relatively new realisation I have developed a deeper respect for who I am. I did not survive my childhood purely through literally and emotionally keeping my head down. I've recognised that I had to fight for being the kind, loving optimistic woman, wife and mother I've become. I haven't allowed cynicism to stain my thoughts or my relationships, which would have been easy. Despite being more broken than I realised, I am in fact the warrior of my own life.

Discussion Points

Dianne talks about her grandson being a trigger for closely held pain. Why do you think that has happened?

What support might someone need as they make sense of something like the birth of a grandchild in terms of understanding their own childhood experiences?

Why do think Dianne sees herself as a warrior?

Note

1 https://www.dictionary.com/browse/connection.

13
Carrie – Strength

I met Carrie while I was speaking at the Buttle UK Conference 2012, where she was leading a panel of young people in education as they told their stories to the delegates and shared their experiences of being in education as children in care, both good and bad.

strength
noun

1. the state, property, or quality of being strong.
2. the power to resist attack; impregnability.
3. the power to resist strain or stress; durability.
4. a source of power or force.[1]

I particularly like the 'source of power' definition of strength in relation to Carrie, although I'm not certain she recognises this for herself yet – but passing through the years will assist her in this revelation.

*

Carrie's Story

I was first involved with Social Services at around the age of nine/ ten when I was recognised as a 'neglected child'. Me and my two

DOI: 10.4324/9781003257967-17

brothers – one is a year and a half older and the other is nine years younger than me – were put on the 'At Risk' register.

It wasn't until I was 11 that I became fostered. I went into foster care a very damaged young girl who felt wholly responsible for my mother's welfare and spent a long time feeling resentful that I had been taken away from her. It is hard to even remember my state of mind at this time, but in reflection and reading reports written at the time by social workers I recognise and remember key points.

I remember being sat down and spoken to about moving out of my mother's, and at the time it was a 'temporary' situation. However, the extent of my damage was assessed and that, combined with a deterioration in my mother's behaviour after I left, determined that a permanent move would be the most beneficial for my development mentally and physically. I've tried to blank out the memory of one of her actions that proved that her children shouldn't be living with her: she slit her wrists when my brothers and I moved out. After she did this she came to where we were and told us that it was our fault because we didn't live with her. She was put in a mental health institution after this event for a period of time.

I have moved on massively from the young damaged girl that I was, but I know certain things still affect me now; but this just means that I have more growing and healing to do, which is to be expected of someone who is only 24.

It wasn't until I was 17 that I decided enough was enough, and I decided I wanted more from life, and to be treated better. At the time this was with regard to my education: my school knew I was a looked after child as I was on a 'special' list; yet, from the supposed support I received from the school, you wouldn't have known. The point I decided I had had enough was when they told me that they didn't expect me to pass any of my A Levels, and that they weren't bothered if I went to the classes and did no work; but I had to attend the lessons or they wouldn't get paid for me. I still now think, "WOW, how the hell did they think saying this to me would be beneficial to either party?!" This was the turning point in my life, which let me move forward and start to heal myself. This meeting happened because I had not been going to my lessons or doing as much work as I should as I was deeply depressed and was dealing with my mother attempting suicide on Boxing Day because 'she had nothing to live for'. I made them aware of what had happened and no support was offered, just an ultimatum given.

I wouldn't ever change my past even if I could. I am the person I am today because of my past, and I have managed to create a positive life from a negative environment.

When I first went into care, I trusted no one and watched every movement of every person around me, trying to read their next move. I struggled with friendships and always felt like an outsider looking in; this of course may have been partly down to my chronic depression that went undiagnosed for years. I could say something to someone and then spend a week worrying about the effect of what I had said, when really the person I said it to didn't even remember it an hour later. This is the negative side. I constantly have to have an inner battle with myself to let things go and not over-analyse someone's actions. The inner battle has become quieter as I get older, and I have gained more self-confidence in my actions and myself.

My over-analysis of those around me lets me read a situation or environment from the smallest of body movements or the way someone says a word. I now use this ability to analyse a situation, then progress personally and professionally. I find it easy to fit into different social occasions, different age groups and from a variety of backgrounds. It is no longer something that hinders me and stops me from involving myself with people, something that makes me become so wrapped up in the situation that I cannot move forward, and doubt every word and action I make.

It is only since I took on responsibility for my younger brother last year that I really started to look at 'what I deserve' when it came to relationships. For many years I have felt lucky to even have someone in my life; but a lot of the time I have put myself and kept myself in negative relationships because I believed I didn't deserve better or didn't really recognise that the relationship was damaging to myself. I am not saying that I have dated men that are horrid, but I have been in situations where I haven't felt confident or comfortable or I've ignored warning signs that things were not right because I haven't wanted to face the truth about certain things.

If I were to think about the kind of man I've chosen to be with, I seem to pick people who aren't straightforward; there is always something about them that makes it difficult to be with them – or maybe it's something about me that makes it difficult to be with me. I could analyse myself all day and still not come to a sane conclusion, and I can hear my family and friends saying: "Don't be bloody stupid, it's not you!" I may not have massive faults but I have seemed to get myself into situations that just don't work.

But this is changing. In the past year and a half I became an instant parent to a teenage boy who had lost his dad very suddenly due to cancer and who had never had much contact with his (our) mother. I also graduated from university and started on a career-creating journey in terms of work. Needless to say, I have grown up. I have had to use the pain and dysfunctional life I have had both to move forward with work relating to looked after children and care leavers, and also in my personal life. I am able to see the positives and faults of my life, and use them to make sure that my brother gets the best from life. Without having this life experience, I do not think I would be able to handle such responsibilities.

The parental responsibilities I have link to my relationships. I no longer just think about myself when thinking about relationships. I think about what effect it would have on my brother, and if it would be positive to both his and my life. I don't mean I'm looking for a father figure for him; rather, I mean the effects of me being happy and stable for my brother.

I do wonder about how my life has changed over the years, and how different it is to a 'normal' life. It has not been an easy ride; but, as I mentioned before, I would not change anything about it. I believe I have been able to create a positive life for myself despite certain hardships, and, who knows, I may have still had a positive life without such things happening; but that would be comparing with something that hasn't happened, and I am not one to dwell on 'what if's'. I take a situation and try and get the best from it whatever the circumstances.

Reflection

I sit reading my words ten years on, aged 33 in my half-decorated home office in my newly purchased house (the second home I have bought), next to my 'Young person of the year 2008' from my Local Authority sitting on the shelf next to me.

Reflecting on my words, life has evolved over the years; my dedication to my brother, my experiences in life then pushed me beyond breaking point, passing through therapy (multiple times) and finding myself somewhere in the mess of it all. Our relationship now does not exist, which I am okay with for my boundaries I require. My birth mum, who I continued to have a complex relationship with, passed away over Christmas 2020. In her death, my grief process has helped to settle a lot of the many unmet needs – re-parenting my inner child, giving her the love, care and consideration that I missed out on as a child and young person.

I am not without family though: this month I celebrate my five-year wedding anniversary with my husband; we have beautiful three-year-old son, 3 dogs, a cat and ELEVEN chickens. Life is so different, my perspectives grown, my soul with so much healing behind me.

I have moved on from surviving (which I was just about doing, even if I did not realise at the time) to thriving.

Life did not just become easy one day – it's been work every day and will continue to be; but within it all I am more centred in myself than ever before. I continue to work on my instinct to be a 'saviour' to others in their times of distress, which has meant moving away from my work for the last ten years, working directly with my peers to support them in transition towards academia (finally). I am sitting surrounded by books and notes to complete my master's degree dissertation (on the accessibility of services for care leavers) with Studentship funding to complete a doctorate. (So much for not being able to achieve, hey?)

I have been sober from alcohol for 18 months, which has been important to my growth ... therapy while not numbing with alcohol is something else, but it meant reaching depths that were deep and hidden, untouched. I did not give up alcohol as I felt I had a drinking 'issue'. I merely woke up one day and wanted to know myself deeper, to stop numbing and *continue* to heal. I knew I had to take the responsibility to myself to do something different.

I spoke about how life is so 'different' from 'normal' in my original thoughts ... Since then, I have learnt there is no 'normal'; that every person I have had contact with in life (care experienced or not) has complexities and have a journey of healing (even if some choose not to take that path). There are of course things that have meant mine and others' experiences have been more complex, but it's not such a lonely place when I recognise everyone else in the world. I still battle with an internal fight of wanting to do well as judged by 'outcomes' set out by the system that I was under (a home, good level of education, stable relationships, a job) and the knowledge that life and being happy and content is actually what is required to be 'successful' for me; but I am happy with my life path and, as before, would not change any of it.

A piece of advice for those with care experience or working with us: give yourself time and space to learn yourself and grow.

You won't get it right, first, second or more times. and it will hurt along the way; but with the vulnerability of not knowing the outcome, or knowing if we will succeed, comes the good stuff – the growth and learning that comes with life. Dare greatly and know that you are already whole.

Discussion Points

What experiences and relationships do you see as contributing to Carrie's healing journey?

In what ways can those experiences be made more accessible to care experienced adults?

In what ways do adult services, if accessed, help or hinder healing from disrupted journeys?

Note

1 https://www.dictionary.com/browse/strength.

14
Pav – Integrity

I came by Pav rather accidentally – not that I believe in accidents of this profound nature. Pav is a friend of a friend, and I had been spotted on Facebook. The friend who had inadvertently connected us had no idea that Pav, someone he had known for a long time, had a background in care. As a very eloquent, articulate, Oxbridge-educated man he defies stereotypes about what it is to have been a child in care, suffering with adolescent mental health issues more than most. Having 'locked down' his experiences for many years, the writing of his time in care was very hard for him to do, although he revealed that he had found a huge weight lifted from him once he had done it, and I felt internally very pleased that I had been a part of a cathartic process by default.

integrity
noun
adherence to moral and ethical principles; soundness of moral
  character; honesty.[1]

*

Pav's Story

It is strange that I agreed to write about a segment of my life that pre-dates my teenage years just as I am trying to control the breakneck

DOI: 10.4324/9781003257967-18

speeds at which I find myself hurtling towards my mid-thirties and the impending dawn of middle age. It is stranger still that I agreed to reflect on memories from this period which I have long sought to leave behind – a time about which my mind has seemingly battened down the hatches so effectively that I am still not clear how I escaped the experience so unscathed – on the face of it at least.

A careful review of these times, in the early 1990s, when I lived in the care of a local authority children's home in a run-down corner of Chorley, Lancashire, in North West England, unlocks many clues about the person I was and who I have become. This is to say that I have never really left my care home experience behind. Not entirely. Equally though, I did not leave my care home experience without some of the scrapes presenting me with a set of invaluable life skills and lessons that I have firmly fixed to my arsenal of survival tools. These have proved loyal companions in an overwhelmingly gratifying journey of discovery, disruption as well as personal and professional fulfilment.

To be clear from the outset, and in the framework of the care home graduate's experience, I consider myself a positive case study of what can be achieved with the right support, coupled with a single-minded determination to succeed and prove the detractors wrong.

During my time in care, I learned the valuable lesson that my capacity to succeed – against the odds – must not be limited by the naturally defensive need to survive in spite of the limitations placed upon me. Instead, I learned to embrace my reality with an offensive sense of courage that would allow me to set myself ambitions that most others could not imagine would be possible within the microcosm of my modest universe.

The hallmark to survival for many in my 'home' was rampant substance abuse amidst predatory emotional and sexual exploitation by external forces who hung around the gates of the 'home' preying on the vulnerability of the occupants within as well as, of course, the unchecked criminality. The casual violence, the misogyny and racism were symptoms of damaged young people calling out for some help and not getting it from those that should have been there, and the substitutes never being enough. Is it any wonder many of us carry scars into our adult lives, even if we learn to live with and mask them as best we can?

I also know that the aggressive racism and exclusion that I experienced during my care home experience helped me to escape exposure to the worst elements because it meant that I could instead turn my attention to books and learning. But even then confusion reigned.

I remember coming across Larkin's poem, 'This Be The Verse'. It was a means to channel my 'anger', only I don't think I had much time to feel anger or grief. I just remember the adrenalin that comes from fear and the need to fight through the grind of a system that spits you out aged 16–18 to fend for yourself.

It would be an almost certain understatement for an outsider looking in at my 'looked after child' prospects to assume that these were nothing if not as grim as the backdrop of Chorley's decaying economy and the socially dysfunctional experiences that characterised much of the community that was my 'home' for more years than I care to remember. Yes, the material hardships were omnipresent: there was no money, there was no support structure to speak of, and there was a heavy emphasis on trying to get me through each day, one at a time, rather than encouraging me to 'waste' my time on the futility of creating a roadmap for a more promising future that was unlikely to be realised. I remember my greatest shock being the profound nihilism and poverty of ambition surrounding me and my prospects. The expectations were so low that it was easy to fall victim to the gloom that was predicted.

How it is possible that all this stands in marked contrast to my present-day self: a Cambridge graduate with a master's degree, the directorship of an international organisation, who spends far too much time in airport lounges and boutique hotels in faraway places. In these days when I am preoccupied with tackling issues of labour law and contractual negotiations in private enterprises, living an incredibly privileged and wholesome life, it still confounds me that I used to worry about how much food I should store away in my bedside cabinet – because it was difficult to know when I might get my next meal, if I had enough money to buy provisions for the week ahead, while the innocuous-sounding 'Independence Training Unit' I inhabited was overrun by care home bullies inflicting assault after assault on me under the partial gaze of in-house supervisors. There were no such things as corporate parents in those days, so there was a clear disconnect from the people the policy makers were making decisions about.

Given all this, it stands to reason that the realisation that I could achieve more was not immediately obvious to me during my early stages of being institutionalised. No one dared to lift my expectations in case they might have to follow it through with some sort of support or action plan. Part of me wants to be scathing about the lack of social support, but I don't feel capable of this because it was also a gradual journey towards seeking a sense of self-identity and self-value during these dark times.

Being subjected to gratuitous and brutal knocks from being a solitary, non-white child in a care home where one's peers were determined to project their understandably misguided anger on the person who least fit, and had the fewest allies in a modestly complex web of care home social constructs and political hierarchies, served its purpose. When I reflect back, it was almost inevitable that I would respond to this injustice with a long-term commitment to challenging bigotry and prejudice. The experience also left me averse to operations which require a pack mentality, where blind and unquestioning loyalty to a cause has to be refracted through a tribal responsibility that might trump the actual interests of real communities of people. The need to do what was right, rather than what was expected, has held strong within me, even when it has proved to be the less popular choice to make. It has not always made me friends, but it has emboldened me to speak up and to make the case for what I see and think without being bound by dogma.

In this sense, I still feel a little surprised that I have managed to survive and have flourished both privately and professionally. Recognition of success ought not to be mistaken for arrogance or conceit. It is not.

When you have walked in my shoes, which have not always been my own, and you have witnessed the things that I have seen, which have not always been my choice or in my interest, then you can allow yourself some flexibility to arrive at a point where you can validate your own achievements and experiences on terms that you define, regardless of what others think. Naturally, this creates a paradoxical situation for others: when they are without any sense of the journey I have undertaken, they can perceive me as a precocious, Oxbridge-educated prima donna, rolling in privilege. I recognise their assumptions because I occupy shades of all those things, but I know there is more to it.

In his seminal work, *A Man of the People*, the Nigerian author and academic Chinua Achebe asked: "What is modesty but inverted pride?" I was 19 years old when I embraced this challenge to be honest about my successes – as much as I seek to be honest about my failures – because it would be disingenuous not to acknowledge the hallmark of my transition from care home experience to where I am now, a place where I share the highs and lows of other 'normal' people, as a place that is deeply connected to my ability to validate and accept the challenges that I have overcome. This is not self-indulgent narcissism. It is a pragmatic coming to terms with the cards life has dealt me and the fact that I have learned to play those cards to the best of my ability. It is connected to the perseverance I have shown in the face of tests that might have broken others.

At my most pugnacious I might argue that the palpable, outward self-confidence and self-belief I exude comes from having successfully jumped through the hoops and passed the tests that society set for me. Conversely, it is intrinsically connected to the contradictory and strategic amnesia that I have had to employ throughout my adolescent and adult life. Just as it was when I was living in institutionalised care – that I was largely out of sight and out of mind – for a long time I have sought to manage this and subsequent traumatic experiences by ignoring them as far as possible. It means that I have earned the right to be the way I am, which, ironically, masks the person that I privately most identify with: a troubled teen with immense insecurities who needs to learn to trust others despite being a thoroughbred survivor who no one can really hurt because the damage has all been done.

Perhaps this is one reason why I have not actively sought to fully reconcile my experiences that rest among the emotional and psychological debris that has littered my life. They spike me like the small and corrosive shards of metal that indiscriminately pierce the flesh after a high-impact cluster bomb hits the ground among dense urban populations. If the wounds from my care home experience had been allowed to fester they would have risked depriving my spirit of the oxygen that was important to both heal and build resistance to other infections. Had I not bound my wounds up and sought safety through reading and self-education, then I may not have survived the experience or fulfilled anywhere near my potential.

In another of his works, *The Education of a British-Protected Child*, Chinua Achebe writes that to answer oppression with appropriate resistance requires knowledge of two types: in the first place, self-knowledge by the victim, which is to say that one must be aware that oppression exists, and an awareness that the victim has fallen from a great height of promise into the present depths. Achebe also argues that the victim must know who the enemy is. He must know his oppressor's real name, not an alias, a pseudonym or a nom de plume.

The reason that Achebe's work will always stay with me is not only because he strongly influenced my personal philosophy of speaking truth to power, no matter how painful that experience must be, but his work also emboldened me to confront my oppressor – fear of dependency and failure – with a sense of permission to speak out about the things that I know too well.

As many children who have been in care will know about directly, or indirectly, from their own experiences, when you are engaged in a jihad – a personal struggle – for your very spiritual and physical survival, without a blueprint or roadmap to direct you, then you quickly learn that self-reliance and self-sufficiency are your greatest assets. The sooner you realise this the sooner it bears fruit in an otherwise trau-matic episode in your life.

While the physical body experiences trauma that can be seen upon its flesh, as wounds that can be seen and rationalised, they can often be left to heal themselves or with modest clinical intervention. But when the soul is subjected to suffering that is often unspoken and invisible, it can remain with you for a lifetime. That pain is dulled with time as you learn to adapt, but it does not go away. Not really. Not ever.

The decision to revisit old ground has been predicated as much by happening across others who, like me, have successfully transitioned from being a 'looked after child' in a local authority care home to 'active citizens' in the mainstream of society, as much as a sense that it is time to speak out.

It is no surprise to me that I managed to get very good A Level grades and went on to Cambridge despite the underlying suffering that has rarely been given a voice. It was what convention demands. But in these times of supposedly 'shocking' revelations about peo-ple in positions of power – from politicians in government circles to celebrities in cultural institutions, right the way across the spectrum to localised actors engaged in 'extraordinary' acts of organised groom-ing that exploit and violate the most vulnerable – I feel it is time to say that I want to be done with hurting and hiding. I want to be done with excusing or proving. I owe my benefactors everything. I owe my detractors nothing.

And at this time when those who wield institutional power, from MPs to the media, are engaged in shrill headline-grabbing tirades about the fact that 'child protection systems fail to listen' to teenagers' voices, at a time when the economic and educational prospects of an entire generation of working-class young people are being decimated, I find myself asking: what is new? How is this different to how it has always been?

For sure, some things have got better, but the voice of young people has always been suppressed or muted. Not because they have nothing to say, but more because the resources that would be required to act on their calls are not what policy makers are prepared to invest in.

The Victorian model of tough experiences making young people strong and sturdy is completely obliterated among young people with different attitudes and values towards work and life. After all, the new generation of young people tend to be socially and environmentally conscious because their life events have been shaped by the economic crisis, global warming, globalisation and the digital revolution. The new forms of technologies and communication that are available have made their experience increasingly global.

And still, despite an abundance of indicators for success to reassure me, I have continued to struggle to find the voice to be able to tell my story about being in care on such candid terms that society might be ready to face up to what happens to looked after children, or how we – in society – so readily allow young people to slip out of the mainstream and face almost certain calamity in their personal and professional lives.

Throughout life I have learned that I do not like suffering to no purpose. I feel that suffering should give birth to something good and creative. So I do not blame anyone. I do not pity or regret my experiences; but I do struggle to get a grip on how I got through things so unscathed. What I'm certain of is that none of it would have been possible without my teachers, my siblings and – unfashionable as it may be to admit – my faith in God, who was often the only 'friend' I could always turn to in good times and bad.

I have long sought to convince myself that I am free from the effects of my pre-, mid- and post-care experiences, but I know I am still haunted by them. I want to say that I've moved on and I keep telling myself that I have done so; but coming back to the subject reminds me that I have not, and I know that I still genuinely fear: my past and my present, and possibly even my future too. As Achebe reminds us, in order to answer oppression with appropriate resistance we must have knowledge, and we must name the oppressor. Fear.

I still experience nightmares about having to sit an A Level French written exam. I often thought this fear was connected to the anxiety that exams naturally provoke in many people; but I actually know – in my subconscious – that this is not the case. If fact be known, I was hospitalised in a psychiatric ward around the time of my A Level exams, and my body was being pumped full of chemicals that harmed me. I recall scenes of my sister weeping at my bedside as she visited me. I remember her asking me to fight what I was battling in my mind and to pull through. Even now, I bite my lip and hold back tears as I recall the tears running down my own face as I sat in my hospital chair facing the fear that I knew myself but I was losing myself. I remember wanting to cry out, but the medication had seen to it that my voice was muted. The powerful drugs they pump into patients put paid to any heroic act of resistance that Achebe writes about. I could not break the cycle of powerlessness and destruction that I was living, and I was not being enabled by the 'system'.

One way or another, I managed to get through this experience of mental ill-health. In a manner that has been characteristic of my care home graduate experience, I have learned how to mask my inner turmoil with an external air of serenity. I have learned to perfect the suppression of what happens within in pursuit of a socially and culturally normative facade.

I compare this experience to 'The Second Coming' by the Irish poet William B. Yeats, who, in the aftermath of the First World War, used religious imagery about the Apocalypse and Second Coming as allegory to describe the atmosphere in post-war Europe. What Yeats described as the "rough beast" slouching towards Bethlehem was the symbol of a new age, while the speaker's vision of a rising sphinx was his vision of the character of the new world.

In my internal world war, I felt Yeats captured the contrary forces at work in my own history, about the conflict between the experiences I had left behind, the world I inhabited and the uncertain future that lay before me. Knowing as we do the trauma of the Second World War, Yeats' prophesying was not entirely off the mark as an allegory to my life, in relation to my struggle to reinvent myself and grow in the face of uncertainty and the absence of cultural capital and economic means.

Over these past months of confronting the fact that I have, in my own small way, reinvented the cycle described in Yeats' poetry, it has been a reminder that despite the 'success' and stability – which are both real and laboured – there is what might best be expressed as my Freudian id's conflicting struggle with my Freudian ego's efforts to suppress in order to make me conform. On the whole, my ego has managed to contain my id successfully, and I have constructed a relatively solid and stable manifestation of myself to the world I inhabit. This has enabled me to make social and professional progress.

In life, from my care home to the present, I have learned that individuals derive strength from their society, and societies derive strength from the individuals who belong to them. I feel like I have built my cultural capital, social fortune and strength with the help of my societies' customs. Equally, I hope that the societies I have inhabited have benefited somewhat from my hard work and determination – despite the starting point from which I originated.

Reflection

Writing my original account was a daunting experience. I had never before found the courage to organise my thoughts about being in care, let alone feel comfortable enough to put my experiences into words.

The reality, and rawness, of what I had buried away for so long meant that I was unable, and unwilling, to make anything other than cryptic references to the abuse I was exposed to during my time in care or the damage it did in the immediate- to mid-term aftermath of leaving care. Not all abuse took place in the children's home; but I don't doubt that living in that 'gilded cage' exposed me to far greater risks from those intent on stalking its inhabitants than I did in the unstable environment I escaped to end up in care.

I remember inviting my loved ones to sit with me as I read my chapter out loud. These were people I was closest to and had still kept a distance from. I remember asking them to let me read without interruption or question. It was the most intimate and exposed experience I've ever risked being part of. Each time was the same. I cried and cried as I read. The tears that flowed down my face were a raw, emotional response to unburdening myself from the anger and pain I felt knowing how easy it was for people – among the public, and professionals in places of influence – to prey on 'looked after' children at a time, in a place, where we are at our most vulnerable and exposed. In those readings my loved ones and I came to an unspoken understanding of what had happened and how it had shaped me and my relationships with them. It reminded me of how my grandparents had similarly sat me down to tell me a little of their own lived experiences in their homeland – India – when it was being partitioned by the British in 1947. It was a rite of passage between me and those who could be trusted with that information.

There are three things I've learned about my personal journey since I contributed to Lisa Cherry's book. *Firstly*, writing about my experience served a utilitarian function for me. Through the prose, I was able to frame my experiences in a way that allowed me to find meaning in what happened instead of simply reliving details of those events to be consumed by readers who I'll never know. *Secondly*, opening up about my experiences made me realise how little I had healed from those traumatic events in my early life. I was holding on to pent-up anger and resentment, as well as great shame and guilt because of my childhood, and I carried the legacy of that time into adulthood. It impacted on my ability to form relationships, my self-esteem and my acceptance of being cared for. *Thirdly*, writing about events I went through played an important part in my healing process. Putting to paper what I would not allow to pass my lips helped me understand what I survived. Ergo, I allowed myself to be kinder, more compassionate and forgiving of myself in the process of coming to terms with events and moving on with my life.

I recognise that the best way – for me – to resolve my issues with post-traumatic events was to process them, not only at a surface level but more deeply. Writing about my personal experiences was cathartic. My thoughts were fragmented and, in some cases, hard to access because they were buried too deep. To piece them together in a cohesive way required some external help. That's why I agreed to cognitive therapy for post-traumatic stress disorder (PTSD). This allowed me to engage in a structured process to continue healing from those early experiences and their legacies. I learned to talk in public and private about what happened. I wrote some more about events. I revisited locations where events took place and acknowledged my courage in surviving them. The writing and cognitive therapy helped me distinguish between original trauma warnings and contemporary non-trauma triggers.

I am not completely at peace with the past, but I do know that I've made real progress. Writing and talking about it has played an important part in my recovery. For this, I'm grateful to Lisa Cherry for the compassionate way in which she has curated these chapters to allow survivors to grow, while allowing professionals to learn from our experiences.

Discussion Points

Pav talks about the challenges of making sense of events and how writing helped him to do that. In what ways can opportunities be given to make sense of experiences, and what might those opportunities be?

> How can you deepen your understanding about the embodied nature of trauma?
>
> What will you do to further this understanding?

Note

1 https://www.dictionary.com/browse/integrity.

15
Siani – Visibility

Siani had found her way on to my website and wrote to me with her story. While it wasn't quite what I was expecting, the relevance of it seemed obvious so we began our discussions.

To have been where she was at the particular time that she was there, with the national media pointing cameras in her direction, and to not be found is an irony too painful to bear. To be so invisible could only create a vibrancy that would ensure visibility.

visibility
noun

1. the state or fact of being visible.
2. the relative ability to be seen under given conditions of distance, light, atmosphere, etc.[1]

*

So this chapter is from the only person in the book who has not been in care. Given that this book is completely focused on the stories of adults who have been in care, you might wonder where Siani fits in.

Siani contacted me initially to share her story and her recovery from years of abuse, and to tell me that she was now happily married and working with children for a well-known charity. I was keen to have

DOI: 10.4324/9781003257967-19

her in this book from the outset, and then discovered that she hadn't been in care.

As her story unfolded it became more and more relevant, I'm sure you'll agree, because Siani lived on the Orkney Islands at the time of the huge scandal where social workers mistakenly removed nine children from their families. It was February 1991 and the raids saw five boys and four girls, aged eight to 15 and all from the families of English 'incomers', taken into care. This raid was a response to talk of ritualistic satanic abuse by a girl from an island family during therapy sessions with social workers and police. What unfolded on tiny South Ronaldsay in Orkney that morning in early 1991 triggered Scotland's biggest case of alleged satanic child abuse. Although the allegations were eventually dismissed and ridiculed as completely false, it still remains known as the Orkney child abuse scandal.

While all of this activity, this huge investigation carried out under the intense focus on the protection of children, was taking place on a tiny 'no place to hide' island, no one came for Siani. No one questioned a thing and, as her story unfolds, the painful irony of it all won't fail to leave you bewildered.

*

Siani's Story

I've never actually been in care. There have been times, however, over the years, when I wished I was. I was brought up on a remote Scottish island, with unconventional parents – my father was 30 years older than my mother, and had been her teacher at school. After they met, they soon moved from the Midlands to Scotland, partly to escape the stigma they faced as a couple with a large age gap. My father had been married three times before, and had himself experienced a traumatic and abusive childhood. I believe that this led to him developing a physically and emotionally abusive personality, which spilled over into his marriages and his parenting – he already had four children by the time he met my mum.

I can see *why* he was the way he was – he was born in 1928 and, in his era, you didn't talk about family problems, abuse, children's rights. If you were getting beaten (as he was) it didn't get flagged up at all. Nor could you talk about your trauma later in life – if you admitted to struggling with mental health issues, it was likely you would be medicated or institutionalised. So my father kept his problems to himself, suffering from terrible depression and rages, passing on the violence he suffered as a child to his wives and children.

As a child, I did live in fear of him. My mum was also quite slap-happy, but her behaviour paled in comparison to his. From literally my first memory, all I can recollect is fear, hiding, guilt, pain and anxiety as he controlled everything about our lives. He regularly fell into terrifying rages which led to beatings and screaming and shouting that could last for days. As we all tiptoed around him in fear he would decide his current black mood was down to one of us – which it generally was. We could only eat certain foods, we weren't allowed to watch telly or listen to any radio apart from local radio or Radio 4.

We didn't attend school. We were all home educated, which meant the only interaction we had with the local authorities was the annual check by the council education officers, who would drink tea and look at our schoolwork, which was impeccable – they never queried our lack of social interaction or unusually quiet politeness to strangers. As well as the lack of social interaction, we were physically quite isolated: we didn't often mix with other children, and, when my parents' friends came over, things were all sweetness and light – he never lost his temper in front of anyone else. I felt sorry for my mum; but at the same time I was very angry with her for putting up with him and not standing up to him. The way she intervened when he was beating my brother, for example, was not to stop him but to rescue his spectacles in case they got broken – we couldn't afford new ones. It was the same when she sat at the doctor's and said that the goat had knocked her over, after my father had pushed her and she'd fallen, breaking her wrist. She was obviously scared of him, cried a lot of the time and didn't know what to do. She was very young (she had four of us before her 30th birthday) and inexperienced, having left school and run away with him at 16.

When I was eight years old a scandal befell the island. A group of families were accused of satanic sexual abuse of children, and several children were abducted from their homes in a dawn raid by Social Services. This was in the days before you had to have reams of evidence before you could remove a child, and they literally took the children on rumour and hearsay. They were absent for months, during which time the island was split into camps of campaigners trying to get them back and the rest who believed 'there's no smoke without fire'. As it turned out, the accusations were entirely fabricated, and eventually the children were returned and many social workers lost their jobs.

However, in the meantime, my father went a bit crazy. He became obsessed with the idea that because we knew one of the families whose children had been taken, we would be taken ourselves, and I imagine he was worried about what we would say if we *were* interviewed. So he did what every crazy, paranoid, abusive parent would do: he sent us 'on the run' for over a month. We left the island on a ferry and took a coach all the way to London, to stay with various relatives. I remember little of the trip, apart from a lot of crying and being ill – for some reason I was sick a lot – and I refused to take my hat off, which was odd because my brother refused to take his shoes off. In retrospect, we were all really terrified because we'd been led to believe we could be stolen away by some evil social workers, so we were both hiding and ready to flee.

While we were away, my father enjoyed the notoriety he received from sending us away. He was a very intelligent man (he's got a PhD and has published books), and he was very convincing in his role of indignant father having sent away his children to protect them (as opposed to the truth – a scared abuser who might be found out). Eventually we went home and the other families were reunited with their children, and the whole thing died down; but things didn't get any easier with our father. He remained as bad as, if not worse than, before.

As I grew up his temper remained, and although he hit out less towards me, his behaviour towards my two little brothers filled me with anger. I used to lie with my ear to the floor of my bedroom, trying to hear what was going on as he ranted and raged, praying that my mum and brothers would be ok. I was filled with terrible hatred towards him, and fantasised about running down the stairs and stabbing him; and in my fantasy my family would be overjoyed about being freed from him, and we'd hide the body and we would all live happily ever after.

The lack of outside intervention in our lives was something that didn't really occur to me until later. The local council never checked up on us apart from that annual visit, and doctors seemed unconcerned. Our nearest neighbour said to my mum one day, "How is Peter, is he ill? We've not heard him shouting in days!" If your neighbour shouted so often you noticed when he hadn't, would you not think to tell someone?! Literally nobody said or did anything. Not my mother, the council, the doctors, neighbours. Nobody.

When I was 15 I began to rebel – cutting my hair, piercing myself, developing strange habits like stealing food and pretending to find money in the street that I had in fact stolen from my mum's handbag. I developed a strange relationship with food, which led to a lot of comfort eating and weight gain that I have only resolved in the last two years! I can now see that all this behaviour was symptomatic of a very troubled youth. I met an older man, a friend of a man who used to babysit us when we were very young. This older man befriended me and, lacking any love or understanding, I easily fell under his spell. To cut a long story short, he groomed me for many months before sexually assaulting me, all under the guise of providing a caring, listening ear. Shortly after the assault, he left the island and was never seen again. And, again, nobody cared or even noticed what was happening.

I left home at 16. I found a boyfriend who was a little older, a harmless kind man who was the first person to treat me nicely. We spent the

135

summer travelling around the country in a car, camping and working at festivals. I met lots of very kind and spiritual people, and began to see how the world worked.

But the pattern of being around an abusive man was not broken. After a couple of years with this nice man, I met a dangerous guy. He was ten years older, a traveller, and a carbon copy of my father: controlling, abusive and manipulative. I foolishly left the nice guy and ran off with the nasty one, living on a travellers' site for a few years, in a caravan, in fear.

Again, I found myself living in terror – not allowed to wear makeup, cut my hair, wear tight clothes, go to the doctor or dentist, drink. You might think it ridiculous for an 18-year-old woman to succumb to such treatment; but, as anyone who has been through parental abuse will know, the pattern was just repeating itself. This man never actually hit me, but would destroy my belongings, throw things at me, stab knives in the wall above my head if I sniffed too loudly, self-harm and blame it on me, shout, rant, rage and threaten to kill me if I left.

Again nobody intervened. The difference between this situation and the one involving my father was that more people were aware of what was going on and still didn't do anything. That was, until I moved to a travellers' site in the Midlands and met a bunch of decent people. One of them gave me the courage to change things. I knew that if I tried to leave him when he was present I could end up dead, so I waited until he was 100 miles away visiting friends, and called him.

I was strong, firm and stuck to my guns, and by the time he made it back I had bought my own caravan at the opposite end of the field and moved all my belongings into it – and had the whole of the site's residents keeping an eye on me to make sure I was ok. Over the years he's tried to get me back, and once I left the site he tried to find me, but to no avail. After a few years he met another vulnerable young woman and abused and manipulated her, getting her pregnant. One day I had a call from an old friend. He was with this girl, who was growing in realisation about the guy, and she wanted to talk to me. I am so glad she reached out to me because I could do what that friend had done to me, and be the person to tell her she could choose a different path. She left with her baby before he could hurt her any more (he had graduated to setting fire to her caravan and pushing her over with the baby), and she is now on her own – independent and strong, and a great mum.

Around seven years after I left home, just after I'd escaped the abusive boyfriend, the growing realisation of everything that had happened began to sink in. I became extremely depressed, suffered from terrible anxiety and sank into a deep, dark place. Once I started having panic attacks, nightmares, flashbacks, I realised it might be time to see a doctor. I was put on antidepressants and the waiting list for some counselling. The counselling was scary, but wonderful – I was lucky to have a very good counsellor who gave me the tools to move forward and begin my journey to recovery. I realised that a rewarding job would help me emotionally, and I worked hard to get a job in a nursery with pre-schoolers. I was determined to change the past and ensure I didn't pass on the trauma to the next generation. After a year, I decided I was ok to come off the antidepressants, so did so – without any advice to wean off, I just stopped dead. This was a BIG mistake, as my emotions went haywire and I went into a spiral of craziness! However, I was determined that, to beat my demons, I had to grow the strength within myself rather than relying on meds. At this time, I had a really dark moment – I found myself standing by my bathroom window, crying, with a craft knife pressed against my wrist. As they sometimes say, you have to hit rock bottom before you can climb back up. I realised I had a choice – give in or ask for help. I texted a very good friend who knew some of what I had been through, and within two hours he was on my doorstep with chocolate and an order: "That's it, you're moving to Worcester so I can keep an eye on you!!"

I moved to Worcester and met a circle of wonderful friends. I got another job in a nursery and started doing an NVQ in childcare. I took one day at a time, and I started to talk about everything that had happened to me. I talked about it all with good friends who had been through similar things. I changed jobs – I started working in a special school, with some kids who had been in care or adopted. I saw their pain and began to help them to see there was a different way to be – they didn't have to follow the path that was set out for them.

I read – a LOT. I read about others who had suffered, and I read self-help books on changing your path. (Two of these books are John Bradshaw's *Homecoming* and Dale Carnegie's *How to Stop Worrying and Start Living*.) Very gradually, my strength grew. I went to university and got a 2:1 degree in Education with Learning Support – I studied modules on child development, SEN, emotional and behavioural difficulties, children in care, disaffected youth, social studies. These studies helped to inform the basis for my growth, as I realised that I was RIGHT – what had happened to me WAS wrong! People SHOULD have helped!

This knowledge didn't cause me to carry resentment; on the contrary, I felt relieved as my beliefs were reaffirmed by my growing knowledge. I determined NOT to repeat my history. As I grew happier, I grew more and more resilient and conscious of the beauty of life. I became brave and strong, and I wrote to my father, voicing my anger and sorrow. I spoke to my mother, and voiced my resentment and regret. Both of them apologised. My mother cried; my father wrote to me. A weight lifted, and I realised that I could have held on to the anger forever, but instead I chose to let it go.

Doing the job I do now, working in a children's charity, I realise that my experiences have been a positive force. I am strong, empathetic, understanding and tolerant to a different degree to someone who has never experienced the trauma I have. I am fiercely socially responsible, and have stepped in during fights to stop them, given first aid to a fitting heroin addict, called the police when I saw a man chase a woman down the street and drag her into a house. I've called Social Services when I've found out about children being neglected. I'm an interfering pain in the arse of Bad Things, and a fierce champion of Good. And if I hadn't been in the middle of Bad Things, and left alone by the world, I wouldn't know what it was like; and I quite possibly would turn away, not see, not hear – choose to close my mind to the abuse, the fights, the neglect and the pain that was happening under my nose.

Experiences shape a person, yes. They can affect you and drive you into the depths of despair and depression. But I always remember I have a choice: a choice to sink or to pull myself up, grow and thrive. I can't imagine how hard it must be growing up in care, and I don't know how my life might have turned out differently if I had. As it is, I don't regret a single day of my life because it has led me to this point, right here, writing this. I have a job I love. I'm married to a wonderful man. We're trying for a baby. I've got a group of bloody wonderful friends who I love dearly. I've got three cats, two geckos and an allotment. I'm no longer controlled by food. I have a big, weird, wonderful family, and have forgiven my parents. And I have the knowledge that I have been through a ton of shit, and survived.

Not only have I survived, but I have thrived, grown and learned much on the journey. I'm now in a position to be able to offer advice and guidance to others who are struggling; and, if the trauma I went through has enabled me to do that, then surely it was a worthy trial. After all, that is why I believe we are here – to be happy and try to make others happy. Life is joy. And, to use a crude metaphor, a piece of carbon is ground around under the earth for a hell of a long time before it turns into a diamond. And the longer it takes, the brighter the sparkle.

Reflection

So much has happened in the last seven years since I wrote my original piece for *The Brightness of Stars*! Where to begin?

I think at the point I wrote it, I was determined to be 'fine' and was bravely moving on with life. However, as deeply embedded trauma likes to prove, sometimes we aren't as healed as we want to be!

After I had my first child, I focused deeply on her and neglected myself. This led to denial of my own issues, both by myself and my then husband, who saw things in the past as just that – over and done with. After around a year following the birth of my daughter, I left him and entered a self-destructive, yet eventually healing, journey of self-discovery.

I had a mental breakdown and went on medication, was referred on to talking therapies and lived on my own with my daughter. Her father had shown himself to be yet another abusive person in my life; however I'm proud that I managed to set boundaries for myself and my daughter by moving out.

After several months of drinking and risky behaviour, starting therapy and meds, I was quite the mess! My complex PTSD, as I learned that I suffer from, was making its presence well and truly felt.

At this time I started a relationship with someone completely not my usual type – kind, compassionate and respectful. He supported my recovery journey completely, and I began a group therapy course for adult survivors of child abuse, run by the National Association for People Abused in Childhood (NAPAC). It was life-changing. Those 12 weeks were the opening of a door to REAL recovery. Following the course, I decided to cease contact with my mother (my father died two years previously) after I tried and failed to get her to acknowledge her responsibility in forming our trauma. I had it all deflected and thrown back at me, and chose then a healthier, happier path without my mother on it. It's been five years now, and I have no regrets whatsoever.

I went on to pursue an investigation into the grooming and sexual assault by an abuser at age 15, and also disclosed to the police about my rape and domestic abuse at the hands of a subsequent partner. Neither of these cases led to prosecution: too much time had passed and there was too little evidence.

However, it opened the door to specialised trauma therapy with an incredible counsellor who I'll always be grateful to.

When I was pregnant with my second daughter I sought mental health support again, and found a different medication. I then went on to marry the wonderfully kind man who I had her with.

In 2020, just before the first Covid lockdown, I gave birth to my son, who was born with a severe brain injury. The perinatal mental health team were there throughout our journey and have only now, after 18 months, signed me off from their services. During my time with them we covered so much. They didn't just work with me on the trauma from having my son Dylan and the events surrounding that; they identified that I had deep-seated trauma right from my earliest years and that there was a lot of work to be done. With an amazing psychologist and several sessions of Eye Movement Desensitisation and Reprocessing (EMDR), I worked to identify and process all the trauma I'd experienced throughout my lifetime.

It was transformative. For the first time in my life it felt as though someone had turned the volume down. I am no longer constantly in fight–flight mode, and I am no longer living with constant fear.

I expressed to my psychologist that I would know I was better when I could attend a festival where I knew my rapist to be working, and not be scared.

Well, I'm writing this just after I've got back from that festival. He was working there.
I saw him.
I was not scared.
I felt safe and confident in my own strength and power, and I had an amazing time.
Now, I truly feel like I'm HERE.

I'm SAFE.
I'm STRONG.
I have taken it all, and it's not broken me.

Discussion Points

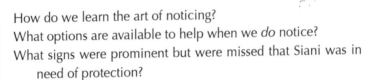

How do we learn the art of noticing?
What options are available to help when we *do* notice?
What signs were prominent but were missed that Siani was in need of protection?

Note

1 https://www.dictionary.com/browse/visibility.

PART THREE

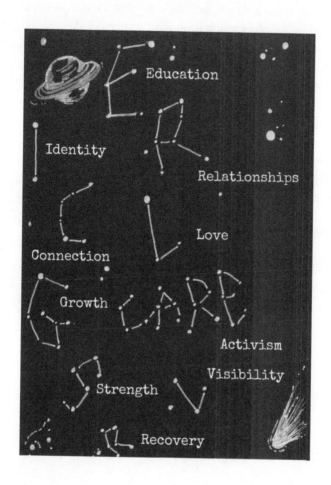

DOI: 10.4324/9781003257967-20

The final part of this book brings us to the present time, with each person sharing from a place of togetherness, having made connections with others with the same experiences. Originally, writing about being in care as a child had felt a lonely endeavour. The ability to connect locally, nationally and even globally with others who share this experience is now an accepted and, indeed, expected idea. Social media has changed everything. This is clearly expressed in the introductions to each chapter as Facebook, Twitter and Zoom are firmly in the lexicon. We are not alone. We were never alone. It's just now we know this, and that changes absolutely everything.

As with Part Two, each story brought words to mind. These are:

Literature
Love
Care Activism
Growth
Relationships

I will introduce each person to you and then leave you in peace to allow the unfolding of a story that will shift and shape and shimmer your thinking about what it means to have been a child in care.

16
Rosie – Literature

Having connected on Facebook (somehow in some group or other) in 2012, we soon decided to meet in person. In 2013 I joined Rosie in Every Child Leaving Care Matters (ECLCM), which was an activist group set up in response to the Staying Put agenda. Staying Put gave those in foster care the right to stay in their placements beyond 18 years old and up to 21 years old, but *not* those in residential care. ECLCM argued, and continues to argue, that this is discrimination towards young people in residential care placements.

Rosie became and has remained a dear friend who I often refer to as my sister.

literature
noun

1. writings in which expression and form, in connection with ideas of permanent and universal interest, are characteristic or essential features, as poetry, novels, history, biography, and essays.
2. the entire body of writings of a specific language, period, people.[1]

*

Rosie's Story

The Stories in My Story

For the first eight years of my life I moved between family, foster homes and residential placements. At eight years old I went to live in a children's home in Muswell Hill, North London, and lived happily ever after; or at least I stayed there until I was 16.

Being in care was like living on a knife edge; I rarely felt safe and never relaxed unless I was reading. Reading was like entering another world where I became the characters and lived out their adventures. It was a safe space, especially when sitting crossed-legged at a local library.

I was born in 1958. Many babies born 'out of wedlock', as it was then called, were put up for adoption or put into care. Adoption wasn't possible for me due to the mental health of my mother and her 'bad blood' which was now coursing through my veins. I had six weeks of life with her in a mother and baby home in Ealing. I was then sent to a residential nursery. My first recollections of life are like an old black and white film slowly coming into focus, the air thick with smog, and 'We are the Ovaltineys' being sung in the background. We are rushing to get my birthday cake, which would be covered in extremely soft, melt-in-the-mouth baby-pink icing. Except it wasn't – it was blue. A lesson in life's disappointments! I stayed with that foster mum for two years.

At four and a half I was sent back to my mother. By then she was married, and I had a brother – though not the son of the stepfather. My brother's dad was British Guyanese. My stepfather accepted him but hated women and little girls. I had the worst two years of my life, and by six and half was severely damaged and traumatised. One sunny afternoon our mentally unwell mother left me, my brother and by then new baby brother in the local clinic and never returned.

Prior to this, my mother often threatened that the police would take me away; I would fall asleep believing that in the morning I would be in jail. That afternoon, I was kept in a prison cell until my baby brother and I were picked up by the stepfather – my memories after this are vague but I do know the older brother was collected by my grandmother. Soon after this, the baby and I were sent to live with a foster family just down the road from my grandmother, and for a short while I attended the same school as the older brother.

The foster parents were middle class, brutal and sadistic. They bred rabbits in the garden, and I absolutely loved the babies. However, they killed the kittens to make rabbit stew. When I refused to eat it, they smacked my knuckles with a wooden spoon, doubling the hits until I was forced to take a spoonful – but was promptly sick all over the dinner table. There were many acts of violence, instigated by the foster mother, carried out by the foster father; it became a sort of sideshow that her and their children would watch.

On returning from school one day, I found my baby brother gone; he'd been picked up by the stepfather's family. Years later when I read *My Name Is Leon*, where a similar scene plays out, I broke down and cried for hours.[2]

I spent time with aunts and uncles, and even some time with my mother, who had another breakdown. I was then sent to a very large children's home in Harlesden, two beautiful Georgian houses joined in the middle by a glass corridor. With about 50 children in all, it was run very much like a boarding school – boys one end and girls the other.

I stayed there for a year, and on the advice of an eminent psychiatrist was moved to a smaller children's home in Muswell Hill. Foster placements would not have worked for me back then; I had no trust in anyone. I was eight years old and stayed in that house until I was 16. Eight years of living on my wits, pandering to whoever was on duty, but in some ways there was stability. I kept the same bed in a room shared with three other girls; not so for everyone – some of the boys were severely abused.

Back in the sixties and seventies my psyche was all about protecting myself from rejection, often training myself not to care. I had my own rules and ways of doing things. I had been told that I would have to leave the children's home at 16. Young people didn't always leave on the dot of their sixteenth birthday, but I was determined that nobody would ever reject me again. As soon as I was 16, I told those in charge of the home that I wanted to leave that shithole as soon as possible.

Leaving care in the mid-1970s was a very different experience to how some young people leave care today. In those days, you left wherever you were living and never looked back. There was no support. I was given 15 shillings (75p) and a tea set!

To overcome the emotional trauma of childhood and a life in care it's important to have tools in your life's kitbag that help. As a child, I was a good reader and could get lost in stories; this was one of my tools. 'Relating to characters is what engages early readers and helps foster a lifelong love of reading. It connects children to the world around them and, vitally, it validates their own reality.'[3] From a young age I was fed stories by librarians: the well-known Pink, Blue, Green Fairy story books featured,[4] as well as parables from Sunday school. It was fortuitous that the books I read often portrayed orphans and abandoned children, characters like myself that I could identify with and, importantly, who were portrayed as overcoming whatever obstacles they faced. I don't remember ever receiving a book as a present, but I devoured whatever was available in my local library. Enid Blyton figured high on the list, the wonderful exploits of children in boarding schools – for example, the *Malory Towers* series of books, where children lived happily without parents.[5] As I grew older, I noticed the lack of any characters in adult fiction with a care background like mine, which for me and others was often mixed: birth family, foster care and residential care. I could, though, identify with classic orphan stories like the determined Jane Eyre[6] or the outrageous Amber in *Forever Amber*.[7] When my difference was overwhelming and there was nothing to identify with, there were contemporary texts, for example, Maya Angelou's *I Know Why the Caged Bird Sings*.[8] The autobiographical text featured abandonment of Maya and her brother by the mother, as well as abuse and cruelty – often the orphan's plight and therefore familiar. Alternatively, I would read horror, like *The Rats*,[9] where, on reflection, I was frightening myself silly, perhaps not to feel the fear and void – that of being orphaned and ungrounded.

When care first left me,[10] I moved about a bit: bedsits, friends' houses, flats, live-in-jobs, occasional derelict houses – whatever it took to stay alive. At 23, I got married and had my first child. I went on to have four more. I got divorced when the youngest was five. My ex had a drink problem, and eventually I had a problem with drink. I do remember that the vibe in early 1980s' society was to be married, to have your children within 'wedlock' – and I did.

In the early 1990s, a couple of years before I got divorced, I started university as a mature student. Before this I worked in something called Prestel, which was a forerunner to the Internet. It looked a bit like Teletext (if you remember that). I was lucky because for many years I could work at home and care for my family. But technology was changing, and having a degree meant I could get a better job and earn more. The idea at the time was that I would study IT. However, once there, and with an idea of becoming a teacher, I changed courses to English Literature and Education.

During the second year, a psychology student friend invited me to give a talk to a group of young girls leaving care. What they told me was that there was no support in place. I was really shocked that, in 20 years, nothing had changed. How could this be? Raging against the system, I undertook an autobiographical project, and after I had finished the degree my tutor encouraged me to continue writing.

Despite going through a divorce and looking after my children single-handedly, I completed my degree. Going to university was the start of the rest of my life. To be on a university campus, to be amongst learned people, to be learning myself, was an absolute miracle in my eyes. I know now that education changes you and can change your life, which is sort of what happened to me. A bit like *Educating Rita*, except of course I was Rosie.

In 2000, I applied for the then new Writing master's (creative writing degrees had only just been introduced to the university curriculum) and submitted part of my autobiography that I had been working on. I was offered a place, but once started was informed I could not write autobiography; it had to be fiction. This unsettled me. All the research and writing I had already done would be redundant; I had to begin again and write a novel from scratch.

During the first year of the course, author Jane Rogers visited the university to give a talk about her novel. Reading *Island* affected me intensely.[11] For the very first time I read of a character with a similar background in the care system to mine. I gulped each page with the ferocity of a starving orphan. I wasn't put off by Nikki's 'sweary' or aggressive voice because I could see through the words to the real person and her vulnerability. Rogers' publishers at the time refused to publish the book unless she changed the voice of the protagonist: 'Why would anyone want to read about this horrible woman?'[12] 'So loyal was Rogers to her character, she changed publisher.'[13]

I read the novel when I was 41. I learnt to read at five years old – this equates to 37 years without any real connection in literature and only the memory of childhood orphan favourites. I hadn't realised quite how isolated or othered in society I really was. Being continually othered in life takes its toll. I was weary of the lonely struggle.

In 2012, I was invited to an event held in a small room upstairs at the Royal Festival Hall. *From Pip to Potter* celebrated the place of orphans in literature, and linked this to the experience of children in care. Poet Lemn Sissay spoke of how some of our best-loved literary characters are parentless children who are living away from home, from Peter Pan[14] to Lyra in Philip Pullman's *His Dark Materials* trilogy.[15]

> How have we not made the connection between the brilliance of these characters (fictional and non-fictional) and the child in care. The problem is not with the child in care but with our perceptions of them and the subsequent treatment of them as a problem to be solved rather than an opportunity for excellence.[16]

This event became a catalyst for events in my own life. That day, I also met Josie Pearse, who was doing a Creative Writing PhD at Cardiff and researching 18th- and 19th-century orphans – e.g., in works such as *Moll Flanders*,[17] *Tom Jones*[18] and *Oliver Twist*[19] – as well as writing about her life as an adoptee, or rather re-writing her life.[20]

Excited and inspired by Sissay and Pearse, I began to explore the possibility of doing a PhD. I knew it would be something to do with care leavers; I just didn't know what. This was also the start of finding my tribe, people like me with care experience.

I'm 63 now and on my way to completing my own PhD in Creative Writing. I'm writing an autobiographical novel loosely based on leaving care in the mid-1970s as well as exploring the representation of orphans and care experience in literature. The origins of *Hiraeth*, my PhD novel, began when I was about 11 years old. I said to my then social worker, *I want to write a story about my life*. A social worker wrote this down and when, in 1996, I applied for and received some of my files from my time in the care system, I was fascinated to see what my 11-year-old-self had said.

When I first went to university in 1993, I was astounded to realise that things in *care* hadn't changed. Another 20 years later, 2013, the government announced that those in foster care could stay until they were 21 but those in residential care would still have to leave at 18. A few of us started the Every Child Leaving Care Matters campaign precisely because things still hadn't changed – and in fact had become worse.

We now have secondary legislation by the Department for Education which states that children in care must always live in care settings – but only to the age of 15.[21] This legal change came into force in September 2021, leaving thousands of children in care aged 16 and 17 in unregulated accommodation without protection. On top of this, we have the English Care Review, which is scheduled to be completed within a year, unlike the Scottish equivalent which was executed over five years and overseen by those with care experience.

Despite the many negatives, there is change, and young people in care and older care experienced people are slowly changing the narrative. But it is sporadic and governed by individuals rather than generic. Understanding that children in care are there because of abuse, sometimes because of tragedy, is the first thing that those who implement policy need to really understand – not just on an intellectual level, but compassionately and empathetically as well as therapeutically. Secondly, they must understand that children need space to heal: a space where children who first go into care undergo therapies that help them understand themselves and give them the tools to live a good enough life. Putting children in families repeatedly and watching as they get attached and moving them on again and again is cruel. And, thirdly, it's essential to understand that the behaviour of those in care is led by trauma. Once this is really understood and worked with, then children in care will have a chance to live fulfilled lives because now it is still luck – luck if you get a good 'placement';[22] not a home, but a bureaucratic place where the language and behaviour around the child is not always conducive to growth or loving support. My experiences in the system have stayed with me throughout my life. I have learnt to have relationships. I have learnt about love – something I didn't have growing up in the system.

I was lucky that I could read at a very young age, five years old. There is a clear line of connection between the relationships I had growing up and where I am today. Aged four, my primary school teacher took a special interest in me and helped me learn to read – this was the biggest gift, and one that has helped throughout my life in my tool kit. There are other gifts in there too: ability in writing, arts and crafts and, when I was younger, making my own clothes. I was lucky I had these tools in my kitbag; but this patently isn't the case for children who don't have and aren't given ways to access them.

Another primary school and another teacher, sandy-haired, freckle-faced Mr H. who told me I was intelligent and would do well. He believed in my ability, and so did I. In secondary school an English teacher, Miss P, supported and encouraged my imagination. After university an English tutor corresponded by letter with support and feedback. And with books as my family and friends, I was always going to have an adventurous, awe-inspiring and love-filled life.

Since starting the PhD I have had the most glorious time. My life has expanded beyond my meagre dreams. I have met and explored care experience with people from all over the UK and abroad. I've spoken about my research at various universities throughout the UK, plus I was a research assistant at Oxford University. I had a great time working with Lemn Sissay on the early Christmas Dinners for Care Leavers; I've curated various projects, including the art exhibition for the Care Experienced Conference 2019; and I helped found the Alliance for Care Experienced People in Higher Education (ACEPHE).

All wonderful stuff; but just occasionally I can't help but wonder what my life could have been like with proper care and support when I was younger, and what I could have achieved at an earlier age.

Discussion Points

Rosie talks about reading as a protective factor. Why do you think that was?

How has that passion for reading helped her today?

In what ways can we think about reading for children as a contributor to healing?

Notes

1 https://www.dictionary.com/browse/literature.
2 Kit de Waal, *My Name Is Leon* (London: Penguin, 2017).
3 Sarah Jayne Mokrzycki., 'The Magic of Harry Potter for Children in Care', in *Transmedia Harry Potter: Essays on Storytelling across Platforms*, ed. Christopher E. Bell (Jefferson, NC: McFarland, 2019), p. 158.
4 Andrew Lang, *The Blue Fairy Book with Illustrations by H.J. Ford and G.P. Jacomb Hood*, Authorized crown edition (New York: Longmans, Green & Co, 1929).

5 Enid Blyton, *First Term At Malory Towers* (London: Methuen, 1960).

6 Charlotte Brontë, *Jane Eyre* (London: Penguin, 2014).

7 Kathleen Winsor, *Forever Amber* (London: Macdonald, 1944).

8 Maya Angelou, *I Know Why the Caged Bird Sings* (New York: Random House, 1993).

9 James Herbert, *The Rats*, New edition (London: Pan, 2014).

10 Lemn Sissay, 'When I Left Care They Said I Was a Great Survivor', *The Guardian*, 30 October 2012, http://www.theguardian.com/commentisfree /2012/oct/30/leaving-care-support-young-people.

11 Jane Rogers, *Island* (London: Little, Brown, 1999).

12 Jane Rogers, 'Writers for Lunch' (Middlesex University, 2002).

13 Rosemary Canning, 'The Stolen Child' (master's thesis, Middlesex University, 2003).

14 J.M. Barrie and Arthur Rackham, *Peter Pan in Kensington Gardens* (Mineola, NY: Calla Editions, 2013).

15 Philip Pullman, *His Dark Materials* (London: Scholastic, 2001).

16 Lemn Sissay, *From Pip to Potter*, Royal Festival Hall, London, 19 February 2012.

17 Daniel Defoe, *Moll Flanders*, Vintage Classics (London: Vintage, 2010).

18 Henry Fielding, *The History of Tom Jones, a Foundling. Edited with Explanatory Notes by Thomas Keymer and Alice Wakely ; with an Introduction by Thomas Keymer*, Penguin Classics (Cambridge: ProQuest, 2011).

19 Charles Dickens, *Oliver Twist, or, the Parish Boy's Progress*, ed. Philip Horne (London: Penguin, 2003).

20 Josie Pearse, 'Backstory: Writing and Not-Writing on the Cusp of Life and Fiction' (unpublished PhD thesis, Cardiff University, 2012).

21 Sophia Alexandra Hall, 'Age of Discrimination: Law Change Will Mean Children in Care Expected to Live Independently At Just 16', *Byline Times*, 9 September 2021, https://bylinetimes.com/2021/09/09/age-of-discrimina-tion-law-change-will-mean-children-in-care-expected-to-live-indepen-dently-at-just-16/ (Accessed 12/9/21).

22 *Children Act 1989: care planning, placement and case review 8 July 2021, c.3*. Available at: https://www.gov.uk/government/publications/children -act-1989-care-planning-placement-and-case-review (Accessed 12/9/21).

17
Isabelle – Love

I am acutely aware that much of what I do now is about passing on the baton to the future, ensuring that I make connections and grow relationships with those who are the next generation to take on the fight ahead. Isabelle shines brightly in all her strength and glory, so much clearer about what she has to deal with than I remember being. We met at a Reclaim meeting. I was dropping in on the Zoom session of this group of care experienced adults who were supporting each other in so many different ways.

The Care Experienced Conference Top Ten messages highlighted the need for more love in the care system.[1] It was number one! Isabelle embodies this in her writing, and it is profound.

love

noun

1. a profoundly tender, passionate affection for another person.
2. a feeling of warm personal attachment or deep affection, as for a parent, child, or friend.[2]

*

DOI: 10.4324/9781003257967-22

Isabelle – Love

Isabelle's Story

Kaitlin Rebecca Mitchell

I'd like to dedicate this chapter to my sister Kaitlin, as while you didn't get to live your life to the full, this book will be forever, and your memory will outlive anyone who had the pleasure of knowing you.

Imagine this: you're nine years old in the back of a social worker's car, speeding around a roundabout, with your favourite teddy in one hand and your oldest brother's hand in the other. You've never been on holiday or left the town you grew up in, so the excitement that your stomach feels is scary and something you've never experienced in your life.

There are two strangers sitting in the front of the car, telling you jokes and stories but not answering your questions or saying where you're going. You look out the window and try to remember every single detail that passes you. Trees. Cars. Houses. Trees. Cars. Houses. DOG. Trees. Cars. Houses. You feel like Hansel, needing to lay down breadcrumbs as you're lost and need to find your way home.

You ask again *"Where am I going?"* You are ignored and told *"On holiday"*, but this doesn't feel like a holiday should. Your mum isn't with you, or your dad, and even though your two brothers are, your three youngest siblings aren't. You didn't get to say goodbye to them either. Why aren't they coming on holiday with you? This isn't a holiday. It feels like you've been abducted by aliens – taken away to a faraway planet where the aliens don't speak your language and you can do nothing about it. Until your brother squishes your hand and says, *"I think we are here"*, you look up and you wish you'd laid more breadcrumbs as you don't recognise anything.

You step out of the alien spaceship and see a house – a normal *(from this planet)* looking house with a curly-haired lady standing outside waiting for you. You go to walk over, but it's like your feet are stuck in quicksand. Your brother squishes your hand again, like a little warmth of *"I think we are safe here."* Your feet become unstuck; you can move again.

You let go of your brother's hand, grab your teddy *(he's called Mr Clown)* and slowly walk over to the house. It feels safe, but not in the way the back of the spaceship or your home felt safe. The lady waves at you. You don't wave back. You were told to never talk to strangers, and this lady (despite feeling and looking safe) was a stranger, as were the two other adults who stood in the front garden of the house.

Little do you know that this stranger's house is where you will spend the next seven or eight years of your life; that, while it's safer than the home you've just left, it's still unsafe. But you aren't able to escape this unsafe house because you didn't leave enough breadcrumbs to find your way home. Nobody ever asked you if you felt safe, or if you felt loved. The time you spend in this house will be one of the most traumatic, unsafe experiences of your life. But you wouldn't know that looking up at this big house with a cherry blossom tree in the front, with the kind, curly-haired lady waving at you.

But this isn't a fictional story, and this isn't something I need to imagine. This was the first day of the start of my life as a care experienced person, aged nine in 2006, shoved into the back of the car of one of the many social workers I was going to meet. I had just said goodbye to my mum – *my dad was nowhere to be seen* – and I was taken with my brothers to this stranger's car. Driven miles away from the place I called home, and left at this strange house, with strangers. I'd like to say this was the only time I was felt like this and the only time I was ever left with strangers in a strange setting, but that would be the fiction in this story.

The time I spent in care was from the outside a privileged one. I didn't move foster placements *(apart from the odd time I was placed in respite care)*. I stayed at my primary and my secondary school, and had a fairly normal upbringing. I had a sense of stability that not many care experienced people have the privilege to experience. But if you peeked inside that foster home you wouldn't see a privileged or a normal home. You'd see a traumatised Isabelle, who felt isolated, alone and completely unloved. This surprises most people, as in all the areas of life I was meant to lash out to show I was struggling, but I wasn't.

The first year I spent with my foster mum and her *biological* daughter was great. I felt loved and had a sense of safety I'd never experienced in my life before. I was able to eat what I liked, wear what I liked and, within reason, do what I liked. It felt freeing. But something changed after a year, and the safety I had in that house quickly shifted into the same level of safety I had before coming into care – which was virtually none.

I'd like to say this was due to me missing my family, my trauma was starting to come out, or that I was just being a typical early teenager. But it wasn't. It was due to my foster mum, my foster mum's biological daughter and several of the "professionals" in my life.

Before I continue *(well I guess it will be you the reader at this stage)* I think it's important to mention that the next stage of this story talks about trauma, abuse and some other possible triggering content around grief. It's heavy to read and digest, so I'd like to make sure you feel ready to read this. Make sure you have a cup of tea/coffee/Vimto, and are maybe in a safe place. Somewhere you feel safe.

I lived within my foster placement from the ages of 9–16, with my foster "mum", her daughter, two dogs and several other animals. If you removed the term "foster" and didn't know my history, we'd have come across as a slightly quirky but normal family on the outside. My foster sister and I didn't look alike, but we could have passed for biological sisters if you briefly looked at us. We were the same age, but went to different schools, had different friendship groups and very different interests. Much like normal sisters do.

But what wasn't normal was how much she knew about why I was taken into care, and how she treated me in response to knowing that. The abuse I had experienced in my biological home was a mixture of both physical and mental, and this was the same abuse I started to experience within a year of living in my foster placement. The only difference was when I spoke out about it to my foster "mum" she called me a liar, when I spoke about it with my social worker she too called me a liar; every single person I tried to reach out to told me I was lying and refused to help me. I even reached out in school, and

I had a single meeting with my head of year, who also didn't believe me. Even in my review meetings when the daunting question came around – *"Isabelle are you happy?"* – I'd lie, and say *"Yes, I am very happy"* because my abuser's mother was sitting next to me and would feed back on everything I said to her daughter. I also knew that if I said I wasn't, I wouldn't be believed again.

So I stayed silent and started to find my own ways of coping – which, as anyone who has ever experienced abuse knows, never works and you end up causing yourself more harm in the long term. I'm still healing and learning how to look after myself due to having to stay silent for so long. If a single person in that time in my life who had any form of power had asked me if I was okay or believed me, I wouldn't have so much trauma on my shoulders as a 24-year-old. But also, if the *professionals* in my life had noticed I was struggling and experiencing abuse, I wouldn't have felt like I needed to reach, "act" out. A social worker's job in my opinion is to notice when a young person's life isn't the best it could be, and my social worker didn't do that.

The amount of trauma I live with at 24 is due to my foster placement; this is partly because I'm at a certain level of peace with my before-care trauma. But the trauma I experienced in my placement I was vocal about, and nothing happened to prevent it from happening. It's difficult to heal from trauma when you know that trauma could have been prevented by the people put in your life to keep you safe. I was "saved" from the trauma at home, but not from the trauma I was chucked into by social services.

I haven't gone into the depth of abuse I experienced in my foster placement – mainly because I'm not ready to talk about this, and nor do I want to in such a public and open way. It's also something I'm still openly healing from, and most likely will continue to heal from for the rest of my life.

The only saving grace for me was school, my friends and my siblings. Two out of those things I had control over; one I again was restricted from, which was sadly also my saving grace in my biological home – my siblings. I thankfully left my foster placement at the ripe old age of 16 and moved back up to the North of England to be closer to my siblings. I was placed back with bio family, which sadly broke down again – but that's not something I'm ready to speak about either. But, as you guessed it, social services did little to notice when I was experiencing abuse again.

I'm the second oldest out of six biological siblings, nine if I include my stepbrothers. All six of us were taken into foster care; my step-brothers stayed within their bio mum. I was placed near my oldest brother and younger brother – their first foster placement was my foster mum's sister over the road – and my three youngest were placed in a random foster home, miles away from me. I didn't know where they were going at the time I went into care, and I wasn't told until a month later when I was able to see them again. A whole month went by before seeing my youngest siblings – Sophie, Harry and Kaitlin – again. The three people I'd been a mum to in my bio home, I was restricted from seeing and told nothing about when I'd see them again. To go from being a mum of three – *at the age of nine* – to being told you are a child, who has no responsibilities, is traumatic and a shock to your system if it's all you've ever known. I was given no support for this. No therapy, not even a trip to the GP.

Nobody asked me how I was feeling when it came to my three youngest siblings, and Social Services made little to no effort for us to keep in contact throughout the bulk of my time in care. This was even more apparent when they were taken into kinship care by my step-grandparents, 300 miles away from me. In their eyes we were now all safe, so why should they keep up that contact? I later found out they had planned to have my four youngest siblings closed adopted – *they had adoptive parents ready to take them* – which is fucking heart-breaking and disgusting. I was nine years old; I knew who my siblings were, and they knew who I was. Why social services wanted to shatter our bond, even more, shocks me. I'm very vocal against adoption for this reason, at least adoption of "foster" children who have family still alive, and ones they especially still have relationships with.

I spent the majority of my time in foster care fighting to see my three youngest siblings. We were limited to seeing them three times a year in a dodgy community centre, theme park or a shopping centre – not places to keep up a relationship with your siblings, let alone form any real memories with. They tried to cut this down to two times a year, until I phoned up my social worker crying and begging her to allow me to see my siblings, to the point I blackmailed her. I say blackmail, but I asked her to imagine if her daughter was taken off her, shipped 300 miles away and told she can only see her two times a year. How would she feel? Now imagine being 14 and having to blackmail your social worker to see your siblings. The bond I have with my siblings has suffered greatly due to this. We've had to work tenfold to bring back our relationship.

But this only applies to my two youngest siblings, as I never got the chance to do this with my youngest sister, Kaitlin. She died three years after I moved up closer to them. So, the memories I have with her are so thin and far in-between. I think it's important to mention that before her death I was already grieving; I'd missed out on 12, 13 and 14 years of memories with my youngest siblings. So, to have Kaitlin die at the age of 12, it shocked me, and I experienced a new level of grief I'd never experienced in my lifetime – something I'm having to heal from to this very moment and will for the rest of my life. Imagine having to grieve someone you have little memories with, and the ones you do are so fictional.

But this isn't a story to talk about the beautiful sister I have, who will never have the chance to achieve her dreams. I could write for years about how beautiful she was, and how that grief impacts me every moment. But I do want to highlight how my PA and Social Services offered no support, other than the pity "I'm so sorry" text message. No call, offer to help me attend therapy, or even offer to take me out for a coffee to have a break from the world of losing your little sister. Just a pitiful "I'm so sorry" text, followed by a misspelling of my name. But that sadly doesn't shock me.

Every single personal advisor/youth worker/social worker I've had in my life has lacked something. Which is love, and treating me like I'm more than an extra caseload. But in their eyes I'm one of them doing well ones, the trophy care child, the one who has a first-class honours degree, will work to change the care child world. I don't need constant support from them. Which is a lie. I need someone to check on me. I need someone to ask me how my day's going or to lend me money for lunch from time to time. I needed that even more so when Kaitlin died.

My local authority gave me all the support in the world I needed practically, but none emotionally. That's the one thing so many non-care experienced people have from the moment they are born. Love and emotional support. Which is what I need more than anything. As in the long term, that's what I'm lacking as a care experienced adult, and that's because I didn't get it as a care experienced child.

Discussion Points

Isabelle has had access to the very latest on offer for those leaving care. Do you think it has been enough?

What would you add?

All the chapters have a word chosen depending on what shines through. Love shines through in Isabelle's writing, or rather what if feels like to experience its absence. In what way can love be present in the care system?

Notes

1 https://info822785.wixsite.com/careexpconf/reports.
2 https://www.dictionary.com/browse/love.

18
Sean – Care Activism

Sometime during 2020 I met Sean on Twitter. It soon became clear that Sean had been involved in many aspects of collective activism in the 1970s and 80s and I couldn't work out why I had never heard of him. A film maker, a policy shaker and a group connector, Sean spent years working behind the scenes to find ways to improve the lives of those with care experience. This included being part of the founding group of the National Association of Young People in Care (NAYPIC). He is tenacious to the end, and will no doubt continue to dedicate his life to care activism.

activism

noun

the doctrine or practice of vigorous action or involvement as a
    means of achieving political or other goals, sometimes by
    demonstrations, protests, etc.

Philosophy.

1. a theory that the essence of reality is pure activity, espe-
    cially spiritual activity, or process.
2. a theory that the relationship between the mind and the
    objects of perception depends upon the action of the
    mind.[1]

*

DOI: 10.4324/9781003257967-23

Sean's Story

My family heritage is characterised by torn relationships and broken marriage, a lineage that is intergenerational on both sides. My birth mother was a 14-year-old Scots runaway, alone in late fifties' London. My errant Irish father had been beaten regularly as a boy, exited into the British Army, where he found brief connection and meaning. He was ten years her senior when they met. A train wreck in the making.

I have been exposed to chaos and violence from an early stage: from my imploding family, my parents' neglect, the true horrors of a care 'experience' and, sadly, into my first marriage also.

We were dumped into care, my three brothers and me, at a very early age – abandoned by our poor-mouth parents to Islington Social Services Department under the lie that our dad had himself been abandoned by his young wife. She however was waiting outside for him. A Voluntary Care Order gifted the 20-year-old, dragged down as she felt she was with four wee bairns, the chance of a swift escape.

But it was my alcoholic, delusional 'father' who, when he left us in the home, left me also a parting gift – as my three younger brothers' keeper. "It's up to you," he said with beery breath on my little face, "to be like a Dad to them" – as he wasn't able to. And so I became, at five years of age, my siblings' 'carer' – a cross I would later bear and a responsibility that has defined me and never left me.

The period I spent in care (1960s–80s) was possibly the most dangerous era a child could have negotiated: state-sanctioned institutional child abuse; staff on a moving platform. It was a time of rampant (female and male) paedophilia. I was literally walking every day of my childhood through a minefield. No accountability existed for residential staff or foster carers as there was little in the way of training, and even less instinctive family-style 'caring' characterised by the 50s and 60s. Social workers (untrained) considered the process of care as 'sink or swim' – based on the mass of ex care that disproportionately, even today, make up the prison population, the homeless, the prostituted, suicidal, teen pregnant, addicted. What I think protected me (and via

me my siblings) from the worst of the predator activities (night-time visits, trawling celebrities, taxi cab outings to under-age parties) was my
ability to speak out. I was an intelligent and vocal young person. And
that made me a threat to those who sought employment in residential
care – when the doors were literally thrown open – just so as to target
the vulnerable.

I think I lived daily for my own future escape and my brothers' also.
Leaving the children's home after a life under supervision and abject
abuse meant more than my freedom. However, I couldn't turn my
back on those I left behind even as my own star was rising. And, having started a degree in Media, I also became a founding member and
key player in the development of the National Association of Young
People in Care.

Historical Activism

The creation of NAYPIC was a major response to the 'Who Cares'
groups run by the National Children's Bureau (NCB) over a short
period in the mid-1970s. I hadn't been involved in those early discussions – the first national representation of the views of young people
in care – but I was on hand to help create our own organisation after
the NCB initiative came to an end.

NAYPIC was the very first organisation that sought empowerment
and representation of the views of young people in and ex care. It
started with less than a handful of us. In London there were just two
people with big ambitions, scheming in a high-rise flat in Old Street.
Within a few years we had developed (my job) local groups in every
borough and most councils in the south of England; similar efforts
emanating from Bradford covered the north.

Amongst my many unpaid voluntary tasks was developing groups
locally. Through listening to young people, via the newsletters I edited,
the conferences I set up, the workshops I ran, I was able to compile
a dossier of injustices and a series of demands. I videotaped young

people across the UK. I concentrated on the things they had to share that could bring change. At that time we had no conception of our individual and collective trauma. I focused on the benefit of their 'lived experience' – on creating answers and making recommendations for improved service. I was visibly moved myself at their stories; sad of eye and hunched in disposition, children broken and desperate to talk but voiceless about their abuses.

But I wanted what they had to say to be unmediated by the audience (social workers mainly). I wanted to take away what was 'known' about them (their past) that would in a children's home normally impact on what they were actually saying. My own experience was that we were never listened to because of what the staff thought they 'knew' about us from our files. Information that we were not privy to that they used to rearrange what we had to say: He's saying that because he's angry after being sent to bed, etc.

The reaction from the huge audience that bought those videos was overwhelmingly that they had never heard young people in care speak that way before. They had. They just weren't listening. They were filtering.

We had secured offices at the Children's Legal Centre (CLC), which invited me on to its management board. This was to be my learning environment as a children's rights advocate, where I picked up my activism by osmosis. I am forever grateful to my mentor and ally, Rachel. The way she taught me – by never doing something 'for' me – was pivotal to all my work and how I have approached any engagement with young people in care.

Children's rights allies are very special people. They seek to empower and not to suffocate true advocacy. Their 'allyship' has been vital in our enfranchisement. I give them due respect here.

Always drawn to the 'creative' in my advocacy work, I created a national newsletter where we had stories, drawings and poems from care. From these sources I developed a series of policies that covered the whole care 'continuum', from assessment and punishments, through to reviews, files and leaving care. Along with the CLC we were invited into the parliamentary group on children in care (1983). Following their reaction, I compiled all the material I could find into a report of our own. 'Sharing Care' was NAYPIC's written evidence. It was highly commended by former MP Renée Short and went on to shape the fundamentals of the 1989 Children's Act.

Our key argument was that young people were legally required 'to be involved in the decisions that affect their lives'. The report also contained the very first mention anywhere of the issues of race, gender and disability in care. It raised, a good ten years before others, the spectre of child sexual abuse in care, which was rampant. I was on the first steering group for Black and In Care, where I brought young people together and made the *Black and In Care* film that led to the formation of the working group – which led to the very first conference. I made more videos, interviewed and supported countless young people who spoke about their abuse: young girls and boys with backstories of racism, violence, neglect and sexual abuse – many of whom made exceptional advocates themselves. Pathways through advocacy were strong elements of the work back then.

Breaking the Cycle?

I put my activism behind me, was accepted into the National Film School and went to Hollywood to work in American TV. And for two decades I focused fully on my career as a TV director, and becoming a family man. I returned to the UK to raise children in an environment that would help them flourish, with a set of committed, loving parents – unlike my own.

But, as I alluded to in my opening statement, violence and abuse were to raise their head again – this time in my own marriage. And for many, many years I lived as a victim of domestic abuse without realising it. And, as my career dwindled and my friends and family disappeared about me, I was committed only to maintaining the outward appearance of a happy family and a partnership and marriage that was seen to be functioning. The reality, however, could not be further from the truth.

I was my children's prime carer. And there were times I had to protect them from the abuse and violence that I soaked up from someone who had deep psychological issues that I was woefully incapable of dealing with and which she refused to acknowledge and seek help for.

When I finally determined to meet with our family GP, my partner and wife decided on the same day to go to a police station and make false allegations against me.

From the initial knock on my door – where four flack-jacketed officers took me away from the two babies I was caring for, one on the potty the other on the sofa in need of a nappy change. From the one-sided police investigation at 2am in the morning, the false (wrongful) charge of assault – with no evidence – to the catastrophic expulsion from my home. Suddenly homeless, childless and facing the shame and disgrace and the loss of my role as family carer and my community position, my human and family rights violated via a secret court – the Multi-Agency Risk Assessment Conference (MARAC). Based on no actual evidence except the word of someone whose sole intention was my removal, her dominance of our home and financial income.

Police maximised charges against me based on historic accounts of abuse (with no proof) so that solicitor and prosecutor could pincer me into accepting a plea bargain and the Crown Prosecution Service (CPS) could meet their targets of male persecutor prosecutions. I refused to barter with them and accept one count of physical assault. They had promised to go easier on me if I did. Doing so would have meant not seeing my children again for a very long time. I pleaded not guilty and faced their wrath.

"Never get tried in a magistrates' court" was the best advice a fellow 'abuser' gave me. This was a man who had himself been found guilty, tagged and ordered to carry out community service.

It was a gorgeous Sunday afternoon. Instead of being with my children, I had been ejected, found 'guilty' on two counts of assault, fined; and, like the other perps (I had no intention of talking to), was sentenced to community service. Meanwhile, the person who had abused me, weaponising the police and courts and using false allegations to further her control, was allowed to stay in our home. The Independent Domestic Violence Advocate (IDVA) officer even arranged to have bars put on the front door and windows. She thought it was to keep me out and her children and my wife safe. The children watching had a different point of view. They saw themselves locked in – and their father unable to help them. I was forced to live in my car, the only belonging I had left, throughout the harshest winter. My (now ex-)wife had maxed out my credit cards; the huge debt I still live with was at that time overwhelming.

I woke one Sunday morning, freezing, having spent the night on a motorway siding, to find the Child Support Agency asking me for money. I was as near to suicide as was possible that day.

For two years the children were left with their abuser. Spartan visits with them in 'Contact Centres' – terrible Dickensian places where fathers like me (most of whom were not even found guilty in a court of law) were all trying desperately to maintain some sort of relationship with their children in just two hour periods every fortnight. The pain that a parent experiences – of forced separation – cannot be described here. The idea that men do not care as deeply for their children or would do anything to get them back is an abominable lie. I recall one of many of these fathers, in his mid-twenties, clutching his newborn baby against his chest crying desperately for just another five minutes with his child.

Children First

It was the loss of my children and their abandonment by Social Services to their abuser that spurred me to fight again for children and their rights; to become an opponent of something I thought I believed in – as, ironically, my own father had apparently abused my birth mother: that it is gender that plays a dominant part in determining domestic abuse. The truth of course is that it is just one of many factors. This politically motivated, 'fixed' position however dominated all thinking and took up all the resources. It did so in my case – at the cost, in my experience, to child protection. An issue not just for straight men (with nowhere to go as victims with their own children) but also for gays, lesbians and those dads transitioning into womanhood who were all caught in a similar position: potential victims without shelter; abused in police custody and courtrooms; denied access to their children – through endless court processes; bound over in Contact Centres and ending up broken-hearted in pitiful support meetings.

I was a so-called 'silent' survivor who learnt that the process was rigged (with targets set on how many male convictions the CPS can tally) and about a criminal and a family court system that is bankrupt. And I died inside. I died a thousand deaths for the loss of my children. The fear I had for their safety. One Xmas eve with snow falling I stood outside the house (forbidden by law) looking up at the windows, wondering about my babies – desperate to see them, to hold them in my arms. I retired to the refuge of a candlelit church that night, to join the other 'outsiders' – drunks and vagrants also excluded from family during the festivities. It was one of my lowest points, and I don't know what brought me through it. The stained-glass image of Christ on the cross; the same image I would return to when the High Court went into session to determine if my conviction had been safe in the first place. I prayed so hard for justice that day. And I got it. The conviction was found to be false.

The period in which I spent away from my children – fighting for my rights and theirs, to be reunited with them and to save them – was the very worst. Unspeakably painful; worse even than the horrors of an abusive, institutionalised childhood in care.

I don't know how I coped day by day. The only thing that kept me going was seeing my children for two hours every weekend, and the thing that near destroyed me was seeing evidence of the abuse on their bodies and being ignored when child protection concerns were raised. The staff in these places – church halls and community centres – were largely untrained and lacked any agency anyway. The social workers I raised my fears with were convinced I was mendacious and trying to get back at my ex-partner; that any concerns about her behaviour were part of the same intimidation and control and abuse I had apparently exercised in our relationship. Because, in all their minds, as a perpetrator, I was just not to be believed.

So here's an awful irony.

Having grown up in care. Developing a movement for change. Working within Social Services to improve things for young people and not feeling in any way intimidated by social workers, I had no fear of reaching out to the Social Services to illicit understanding and get help and support for my family.

The first time I arrived at the local Social Services office in Bristol South was to raise child protection concerns. I had at that time been arrested for domestic violence and abuse (DVA) but not been in a court of law, had not been found guilty. The family in my absence had been designated a social worker, but she refused to take my calls; hence the meeting. As I waited for her and the Area Team Leader I looked up at the wall and saw this:

A Charter For Looked After Children.

A lengthy list of promises to those in care. Quite extensive. It was a vindication; everything that I had worked for back in the day. It included the right of children to be heard and to be involved in decisions that affect their lives.

It was sadly, however, also a symbol of the gulf that existed between myself, the family social worker (who had already determined I was a perpetrator) and the Social Services team leader – people who knew literally nothing about me; unaware of my past and the work I had done. They knew nothing about the background of my wife, her serious mental health issues, or about the abuse that had been occurring for years within my family; the impact my ex-partner's mental health had on me and the children. Except they thought they did.

"Your wife tells me you grew up in care," the team leader said to me at one point. I had taken my aunt with me as support. She looked daggers back at the man. "What does that have to do with anything?" I replied. "Well, it's just that your wife has her issues, and you have yours. What with you being brought up in care ..."

Outcomes

It was a full year later that I managed to overturn the wrongful conviction in the High Court, with the help of a female barrister who was more than willing to ask the defendant difficult questions – questions that no one had been prepared to ask to date. The courtroom gasped aloud at the responses and unguarded reactions as it became clear my ex had lied about her abuse. The IDVA officer who had supported her actually squirmed in her seat. The same woman who had abused me in a magistrate's court and been instrumental in keeping my children from me for 12 months. A policewoman in the dock kindly offered me a hanky. The judge made a swift decision – in my favour. I thought great, now I can see my children again. However, the ruling had no bearing on the Family Court and the Children and Family Court Advisory and Support Service (CAFCASS).

It took me a further year through a Family Court to prove serious child protection concerns were true and to be given sole custody (residency) of my three children. What an awful place, secretive and punitive, that sets parent against parent – and where children get no say over their own lives. A judge who is as removed from real life as it is possible to get, to the children's lawyers who stretch out a case as long as they can, the barristers and solicitors. These professionals who all come from the top tiers of class privilege: they really are the only ones to benefit – financially – from the most pitiful levels of human misery.

No one is ever accountable: not the police or MARAC, or the Social Services who set the ball rolling with their false narrative; the family social worker who visited a handful of times, whose gendered approach saw her supportive of a child abuser, who also advised the area Health Visitor and the nursery and the junior school that I must not be allowed to see my children.

My eldest son was in his final year of junior school. He produced drawings where he was being beaten around the head at home. It was these that finally made it into a courtroom and changed the whole tenor of the case.

CAFCASS – the court-appointed social work service – had determined to leave the children in our lovely family home, which was being defaulted on and in an ever-growing state of mess, even after I was found not guilty. It was a slow process to bring these 'professionals' around, To convince them I was the parent most able to bring the children up. And if I hadn't secured a house with two spare rooms it may have taken even longer. I am grateful both to a probation officer who believed me (and told me I didn't have to attend DVA classes) and to a housing officer who had himself been a silent victim of violence from a girlfriend. He was able to provide me with a council flat, accepting I was a victim despite the courts. He told me that he woke up one night and found his girlfriend hovering over him with a bread knife in her hand.

I have cared for my children full time as a single parent these last ten years. My ex-wife is not allowed access. But I am lucky that I now have a wife who is a brilliant mother to them – a woman who also experienced DVA in her previous marriage. We love and support each other as married couples should.

I used the time they were at school (the same school that had denied me access to my own children) to set up a charity to support so-called 'silent' groups within domestic abuse. I began direct talks with the same police force that wrongly arrested me. It took an exceptional officer at Avon and Somerset Constabulary who, with my help, altered their approach to domestic abuse. He also made a public apology to me on national radio. Very moving. The local council that had secretly established a gender-biased policy that set the police against me then today no longer have 'targets' I am glad to say. Their policies are inclusive. And, as for the Social Services Department that failed my children, I wouldn't go near them again – not ever.

And there have been times when I could have done with their support. To help both myself and my children cope with the trauma inflicted upon us – by them.

I am, however, grateful to those incredible women (mostly) who stayed with me and who went against the prevailing ideology and punitive system. A neighbour, Trudy, who attended the police station to enquire after me when I was arrested; who told the police and the Social Services that they had clearly got it wrong and was ignored. My probation officer, Sue, who was so very kind to me, who believed me. Helen Battrick, my solicitor in the Family Court who said she was more used to supporting women against men but who backed me all the way. When you are a male demonised wrongly as a wife beater by the whole of society, I found it is vital to have female support – that other women believe in you.

Working Together within Practice

All of us – the social work profession, educators, neighbours, DVA practitioners and policy makers (including Women's Aid and Safe Lives, the Association of Chief Police Officers and the police, the CPS, judges, politicians, legal professionals, those in health care, training bodies, researchers and university staff, council service staff, Police and Crime Commissioners) – are obliged to put our prime responsibility towards child protection ahead of uncritical support for DVA victims.

It is clear to me that systems can change over time. Good practice is not static. And the professionals need to be open to 'lived experience' and to learn from those who know best. We need to develop an alternative, holistic and inclusive approach to domestic abuse; one favoured by the woman who established the Refuge movement in Chiswick in the 1960s: a Christian woman who was at the fore of what has become a national movement, and who recognised that both sexes (and others on the gender line) can be violent and controlling. And that it is the children that must come first.

Erin Pizzey was absolutely pivotal to my understanding of what was happening to me at the hands of those in professional practice during the period of my family crisis. Erin saved me and my family with her support and guidance. Erin Pizzey sorely needs to be listened to. She also deserves a public honour for her incredible contribution firstly to women and, latterly, to male victims of DVA. Family therapy is crucial: community-based services that seek to assist even the abusers (who will have childhood issues of their own) rather than excommunication. There is a sense of a thirst for vengeance, not unlike public floggings, within the public's and the professionals' desire to isolate, humiliate and penalise 'perpetrators' of DVA.

The simplistic notions that cement DVA policies and practices, the wider public's attitudes also, need if not a total overhaul then a moving on, a development of support outwards to a broader, more inclusive base. We need, in essence, to be aware that anyone is a potential victim of DVA and/or intimate partner violence (IPV) across society, *regardless* of age, *gender*, race, *sexuality*, wealth, and geography. And there has to be a fairer use of resources so that, for instance, men with children can find solace and escape from harm in the home. And the issue should be one of family therapy and child protection combined and not viewed in a binary way, solely through a gendered lens. We must remove ANY impediment to child protection, and at all times and at all stages place children first and allow them, where possible, to speak freely for themselves.

Discussion Points

In what ways was Sean met with assumptions and prejudices? How can our own assumptions be observed safely and with support rather judgement?

> What opportunities of safely reflecting upon your own assumptions do you have?

Note

1 https://www.dictionary.com/browse/activism.

19
Jamie – Growth

After being loosely connected in various social media spaces, Jamie and I finally met in person at the Care Experienced Conference held in Liverpool in 2019. Having read the original first edition of this book a few weeks earlier, and a keen listener on the *Trauma, Resonance, Resilience* podcast, Jamie invited us to collaborate on a workshop. We went on to co-facilitate a workshop for therapists in recognition of the lack of available wisdom to those in the field of care experienced adults and what they might bring to the therapy room.

> **growth**
> *noun*
> the act or process, or a manner of growing; development; grad-
>   ual increase.[1]

*

Jamie's Story

A Child of the State?

I was born in the early 1980s. The three names on my birth certificate were given to me by my birth mother on the day I was born when, in a semi-conscious state, she was asked by a social worker what she

DOI: 10.4324/9781003257967-24

would like to call me. The day after a Place of Safety court order was sought for me to be placed with a foster family, due to concerns about the potential impact of my mother's mental wellbeing on my early development. I was placed in foster care at a week old with the same family as my half-sister, who had been fostered two years earlier. We remained with the same family in foster care until we were 18.

When I share this aspect of my care story with other care experienced people and professionals there almost always follows a surprised gasp: *"Your story is rare."* Rare perhaps, due to the lack of legal or practice definition of long-term foster care until it was formalised legislatively by the English government in 2015.[2] Yet my story shows the effects of long-term foster care "are lifelong, and the resulting task of building an identity and a coherent life story must be addressed in different ways as life progresses" (Barratt and Lobatto 2016, p. 268).

I have no memory of childhood contact with my birth parents or my other half-siblings. However, I received frequent visits, inspections and checks by social services into all aspects of my life, with everything documented reminding me that ultimately I am "a child of the state" (Sissay 2012).

A Place at the Table

I grew up in a working-class foster family in social housing on a council estate in North London. Both parents worked in factories, handing over between day and night shifts to take care of their two biological children, my sister and me. We were cared for and treated equally, both the good and the struggles. I vividly recall the scarcity and worry imbued in the troubled Thatcher years of unrest and recession when warming our house was a luxury, not a necessity.

The earliest memories of my childhood are sitting around the table – the first as a toddler, perhaps two years old. It's around 6am. Dad is getting ready for work. He carries me downstairs, and I watch as he heats milk in a pan for my cereal. We sit, eat and toddler speak. Like the milk, those mornings at the table together were full of warmth.

The second memory, still a toddler but a little older: our family of six sitting around the table finishing Sunday lunch. I recall fragments of words and emotions: *"Your mum wasn't well. We fostered you both. You are part of our family."* My sister found her tears, our foundations pulled out from under her. Too young to comprehend, I felt the shared warmth around the table holding on to the safety of that table.

The third memory is a Sunday dinner not long after. *"We're separating. He's moving out."* It happened in a blink. I remember shouting, and Dad's tears of confusion unavoidably mixed with ours. I lost my hold on the table, and home lost its sense of safety and belonging. From that tender age, I began a gradual retreat into myself.

Being working class and their separation meant adoption was never an option.

Multiple Transgenerational Transmissions of Trauma

They were the yin and yang of parents. Dad brought warmth and playfulness, and Mum rigid structure and a chill discipline. I recognise now my longing for connection and warmth; yet in working those tough, long hours as a single parent she had little to give. Inevitably our relational dynamic triggered an unconscious conflict of belonging in me that I now understand to be my "primal wound" (Verrier 2011) of unacknowledged trauma embodied in my early separation from my mother at birth.

An important part of my trauma healing as an adult has been to explore and reflect on all my parents' stories, to empathise and make peace with our early relationships. There is little recognition given to the intergenerational narrative and historical trauma of foster parents that might influence parenting. Mum was born in 1950s' Pakistan five years after partition. Her mother, a schoolteacher, and her father, who worked in government, were reserved and disciplined, expecting obedience. I recall, as a child, overhearing the rare emotion of Mum's anguish at being unable to stand up to them, and this was the same discipline and avoidant attachment pattern re-enacted in our relationship. I find myself wondering what it was like to be born and live as a British female child within the fracture and trauma of post-partition Pakistan, straddling two cultures and two possibilities for being a young woman. I find resonance in what it feels like to straddle multiple narratives and families in my care experience.

At the age of 27, when I sought access to my care records, I asked if I could access my birth mother's files too as I knew so little about her or my birth family history. My request was accepted. I recall attending the social services office, where a warm social worker from my childhood handed me a number of large files. I could intuitively feel her deep sadness as to what I was about to read as she sat with me briefly to explain that some information was redacted and offered to answer my questions. As is the case for many care experienced adults, I was not offered therapeutic support.

I learnt that my mother had experienced significant systemic trauma never shared with me or my siblings (Crabb 2020). She had been controlled and misunderstood by her parents. Equally, her husband lacked the empathy she needed following a stillborn child that led to depression and his abandonment. This lack of care triggered enduring mental health challenges. She experienced significant harm from psychiatric drugs. At the age of 37 I travelled to Australia to meet her brother, my uncle, who shared a letter in which she describes the trauma of electroshock treatment. There was no evidence of the relational support she truly needed. She hid her pregnancy with me up until two months before my birth, fearful of my removal. Both my mother and my uncle pursued contact throughout our childhood, which was refused.

Why was her story so clearly documented by social workers and professionals, and attempts at contact never shared with me? Why had it taken me to find the files, and my uncle to uncover the truth of her love for her children even in her difficulties? I buried the files away with my sadness and rage.

During my childhood there was little, if any, discussion about my birth family. My struggles were permeated by what Goodall (2005) describes as "narrative inheritance" of stories passed or not passed on to children about their families. I was told that my mother was unwell, damaged and could not look after her children. That disembodied narrative left only space for me to create fantasy, fearful of the spectre of a mother who was sick and did not care. In her brilliant TED Talk 'The Danger of a Single Story' (2009), novelist Chimamanda Ngozi Adichie warns that, in hearing only a single story about another person, we risk a critical misunderstanding that is potentially harmful. With a lack of a coherent narrative, struggles with my mental wellbeing came to pass.

One Caring Adult

Seeing Dad at the weekends, and his kindness, brought comfort. Yet my return home churned with overwhelming anxiety as my relationship with Mum became strained as we battled to be ourselves, misunderstanding each other and our unmet needs. I began to struggle with outbursts of anger, distress, depression and anxiety. Night terrors followed, together with inconsolable outbursts at home and at school. So began my story of one caring adult: teachers, throughout my late primary and secondary school. In contrast to home, my teachers were empathetic, gave me individual time and recognised there was more to my distress than my behaviour.

Concerns about the possibility of the hereditary nature of my difficulties led to a psychologist referral. She was a kindly middle-aged woman, but it felt like I was being studied like the tiresome questionnaires I had to complete for social worker reviews that led to little. She invited me to explore my birth family, but I froze and could find no words. Her invitation to draw a picture felt like an intrusion to a place unknown and protected. Perhaps if she had shared some of her vulnerability I may have melted. My care records reveal that in an adjacent room Mum was asked whether she understood my struggles were likely due to my birth separation, but no recognition followed. Soon after, a family member visited my bedroom with a stereo and offered a deal: *"If you stop playing up, you can have it."* So I practised what I was taught: to swallow and lock away my emotions.

A Double Loss

As I reached my teenage years a new social worker visited. She shared news of my half-brother, who had been adopted and was exploring contact. It triggered confusion in me. It was a tough period to be my social worker as a few weeks later she delivered news of my birth mother's death and, two weeks after, my brother's suicide. I recall her visible sadness and tears during the visit as she conveyed the news with empathy. I did not know what to do with her emotions or my own. This genuine attempt at relational connection rattled Mum. The social worker was never to return. It was as though these losses were not significant. No one took my hand to go to the funeral. I learnt that if I had, I would have met my uncle and my brother whom his adoptive mum shared in a letter, *"He would have loved a brother."*

How do you grieve the loss of people you have never met. How do you grieve the loss of the longing to meet them?

Leaving Care and University

Leaving care at 18 was an implicit and mutual understanding between Mum and me. From my early teenage years I was prepared for independent living. My drama teachers were undeniably my significant caring adults at this time. They basked in my creativity, mirrored my infinite potential and encouraged university, and I was accepted to study drama and education. I felt like an outsider from my middle-class peers, who, supported by their parents, did not have to work. I found solidarity with a small group of working-class peers. I moved into a flat on the top floor of a council block and worked in a shop to get by. It was exhausting but I embraced learning and the freedom to become myself. The hard graft paid off and I graduated with a 2.1.

Feeling Queer

After school I remained in contact with a teacher who became a friend. She came out to me as being in a relationship with a woman, and I was invited for her birthday at a queer club. It was camp, fun and colourful, but being followed around by a guy was confusing. Collecting my jacket to leave, he appeared and as he leant in to kiss me I found myself obliging. I remember feeling dizzy and confused as I left.

The next day I realised that sexuality was knocking at my door, which prompted my exploration of gay London. During this time at university I was introduced to feminism, queer theory and activism by a queer, care experienced lecturer – another supportive teacher. Initially I was mesmerised by the glitter and the potential of community of the London scene. Yet the part of me that was desperate to belong ultimately led me to feel harmed and abandoned by the artifice, transactional relationships and addictions. A dark night of the soul where I lost control ultimately led me to embrace queer as my identity. Being care experienced, an outsider who longed for love, a home and inclusive community, queer politics just fit. Jack Halberstam reflects *In a Queer Time and Space* that queer theory "has the potential to open up new life narratives and alternative relations to time and space" (2005, p. 2). A queering of family offers a lens for exploring the multiple possibilities of what family can be, questioning normative ideologies and constructs of the family that ultimately stigmatise those impacted by the care system.

Thankfully coming out was uneventful and mostly supportive. My timing meant I did it on my terms. I remember I had resolved that if the family did not accept me I would just get on with life on my own terms. That feels like a strange reflection now, and I recognise it was a learnt ability to emotionally disconnect to protect myself.

Learning Differences

My work life could be described as a squiggly line with a common theme of people and relationships. After university I applied for an admin position in a community project with struggling young people. My manager was the first person who truly saw me, acknowledged my care experience with empathy, and encouraged me to embrace and take the first steps to explore my birth family story. When the project ended I was encouraged to apply for a lecturing position at my undergraduate university. The competitive narcissism of middle-class academics and the challenge of teaching adults triggered imposter syndrome. I survived those nine months in my sympathetic nervous system. I leant into my strengths, encouraging students to explore outside of the box, facilitating group work and taking care of students who had additional needs and wellbeing challenges.

I decided a master's degree would support my career but, after a few months, dropped out. The level of academic-speak went over my head, frazzled my brain and triggered overwhelm, and so it shut down as it had at school. I carried shame and failure in my body. I tried a different course a few years later and felt the paralysis again. Thankfully a colleague asked, *"Do you think you might be dyslexic like me?"* That important question led to my diagnosis of dyspraxia and dyslexia, and a journey of self-discovery. My story is not an isolated example. I have met multiple care experienced people who were diagnosed with learning differences and neurodiversity, significantly after leaving care. We need to ask to what extent a predetermined focus on care experienced people's behaviours and the paradigm of mental health overlooks the potential of undiagnosed learning differences and neurodiversity (Eden and Crabb 2021). With the support of an empathetic specialist tutor, I began to reframe the struggles I experienced at school. They helped me develop confidence and strategies, and referred me to an empathetic counsellor who explored with me that important trauma-informed question *"What happened to you?"* If you can, watch the amazing film *Like Stars on Earth* (Khan and Gupte 2007). It embodies an important message in my story of how significant teachers can be for care experienced people and those with learning differences.

Vulnerability and Healing Relationships

I struggled significantly with relationships without example, guidance or support. Meeting loss and vulnerability, including cancer diagnosis and recovery, led me to stop and take stock of and consider a more mindful direction in my work, inspired by how relationships had supported and enabled me. I trained in learning differences, neurodiversity and disability support, and worked as a university disability coordinator and with the Diversity and Ability (D&A) enterprise, working with hundreds of amazing students alongside the most brilliant caring team and diverse community. These roles led me to embrace the power of authentic and enabling relationships. To deepen my understanding I began counselling and psychotherapy training.

My therapy training helped me understand the language of attachment, relationality and trauma. In tandem, my personal therapy supported an embodied relational exploration of my care experience. My therapist was vulnerable, named her mistakes and engaged in repair, and helped me explore how my trauma lingered in my body, understanding healing from the inside out. Equally, the group process offered an experience of community with whom I could feel safe to share my story and feel collective healing. Karen Treisman (2017) importantly recognises "relational trauma requires relational repair". Undeniably it was mutual relationships that supported my post-traumatic growth (Schwartz 2020), and this lived experience of relational healing informs my relational and trauma-informed practice as a psychotherapist.

From one Caring Adult to Community and Collective Healing

In his reflective account of his experience of foster care, Josh Shipp (2017) recognises how "every kid is one caring adult away from being a success story", as I hope is reflected in my story. Whilst I can share many more aspects of harm, the greatest harm was how my story was denied at the times I needed it the most. We must recognise how multiple transgenerational transmissions of trauma for care experienced people are likely. Hence therapeutic work that is trauma-informed, relational and sensitive to told and untold stories is crucial. I am blessed with the support of the Aashna Counselling and Psychotherapy community to hold space to develop this work.

Joining the Care Experienced Conference (2019) team created the opportunity for me to experience intergenerational relationships and a sense of kinship and mutual healing in both the sharing of our stories and recognising the creativity of our resilience. Equally, this has been my experience as one of the many members of Reclaim Care, a collective of care experienced people focused on healing together, supporting each other, understanding our shared histories and imagining possible futures. These relationships have been life-changing. It has led me and other care experienced people to ask why it took us until adulthood to feel this sense of community belonging. The elephant in the room is the legacy of systemic discrimination, shame and stigma that has historically prevented our process of coming together as a community to understand and heal our collective trauma (Hübl 2020) as other minority groups. Healing the legacy of our care experience lies in relocating agency in the collective and recognising relationships as the locus for change (Relational Activism 2021).

Drawing from my story, therapeutic and community work, I am calling on those engaged in the care system and our community to embrace these key reflections:

1. One caring adult can be transformative in supporting post-traumatic growth; and, equally, it takes an intergenerational community for our collective healing process.
2. Care and sensitivity to support us to explore our multiple stories and narratives can mitigate the impact of transgenerational trauma.
3. Understand, embrace and support our explorations of intersectionality where support can help us to scratch below the surface of our care experience.

4. Recognition and celebration of our multiple narratives and inter-sectionality can provide multiple possibilities of community support and healing.

Discussion Points

Why do you think the decision was made to keep Jamie oblivious to the contact that his mum so desperately tried to have with him?

How might contact have helped him in his journey of understanding why he was in care?

Jamie asks the question in his story: To what extent does a predetermined focus upon care experienced people's behaviours and the paradigm of mental health overlook the potential of undiagnosed learning differences and neurodiversity?

Notes

1 https://www.dictionary.com/browse/growth.
2 Care Planning and Fostering (Miscellaneous Amendments) (England) Regulations, http://www.legislation.gov.uk/uksi/2015/495/pdfs/uksi_20150495_en.pdf.

References

Adichie, C.N. (2009) The Danger of a Single Story https://www.ted.com/talks/chimamanda_ngozi_adichie_the_danger_of_a_single_story.

Barratt, S. and Lobatto, W. (2016) *Surviving and Thriving in Care and Beyond: Personal and Professional Perspectives*. Systemic Thinking and Practice. London: Karnac.

Care Experienced Conference (2019) The Care Experienced Conference: Past, Present and Future http://careexperiencedconference.com/.

Crabb, J. (2020) Her Name Was Jean: International Women's Day 2021. Jamie Crabb Therapy https://www.jamiecrabbtherapy.com/post/international-women-s-day-2021-her-name-was-jean.

Eden, L. and Crabb, J. (2021) A Hidden Intersectionality: Care Experience, Disability and Neurodiversity. Diversity and Ability (D&A) https://diversityandability.com/blog/a-hidden-intersectionality-care-experience-disability-and-neurodiversity

Goodall, H.L. (2005) Narrative Inheritance: A Nuclear Family with Toxic Secrets, *Qualitative Inquiry*, 11(4), pp. 492–513.

Halberstam, J. (2005) *In a Queer Time and Place: Transgender Bodies, Subcultural Lives*. New York: New York University Press.

Hübl, T. (2020) *Healing Collective Trauma: A Process for Integrating Our Intergenerational and Cultural Wounds*. Boulder, CO: Sounds True.

Khan, A. and Gupte, A. (dir.) (2007) *Like Stars on Earth (Taare Zameen Par)*. Aamir Khan Productions, PVR Pictures.

Relational Activism (2021) Relational Activism https://www.relationalactivism.com.

Schwartz, A. (2020) *The Post-Traumatic Growth Guidebook: Practical Mind-Body Tools to Heal Trauma, Foster Resilience and Awaken Your Potential*. Eau Claire, WI: PESI Publishing & Media.

Shipp, Josh (2017) *The Power of ONE Caring Adult* https://www.youtube.com/watch?v=u_Oapo1Q7_w.

Sissay, L. (2012) A Child of the State https://www.ted.com/talks/lemn_sissay_a_child_of_the_state.

Treisman, D.K. (2017) *A Therapeutic Treasure Box for Working with Children and Adolescents with Developmental Trauma: Creative Techniques and Activities*. Illustrated edition. London and Philadelphia: Jessica Kingsley.

Verrier, N.N. (2011) *The Primal Wound: Understanding the Adopted Child*. London: British Agencies for Adoption and Fostering (BAAF).

20
Shaunna – Relationships

In acknowledgement of the particular challenges facing care experienced academics, the group Alliance for Care Experienced People in Higher Education (ACEPHE) was formed in 2019.[1] This has been another online space of great wisdom and support. As a PhD student I attended its first meeting and met the incredible Shaunna.

relationship
noun

1. a connection, association, or involvement.
2. connection between persons by blood or marriage.
3. an emotional or other connection between people.[2]

*

Shaunna's Story

When I was a young girl I always thought relationships were permanent. I viewed my mother, father and sister as people who will always be in my life. We often think of relationships, especially family, as beacons of support and love. These feelings carried me through difficulties I faced as a young girl. However, when I was ten years old I looked around my front living room and recognised that these relationships

DOI: 10.4324/9781003257967-25

were not as secure as I wanted them to be. At this point we lived in a council house in Wigan; we didn't have much but we had each other. I looked around at ten years old and found my grandparents, cousins and family friends had already passed away. Then, at that moment, I felt this feeling of loss, displacement and longing for them. I started to feel the fear that these people I love may not always be around. It is silly as, when I was two years old, my mother, the most beautiful soul in my life, was diagnosed with terminal cancer. I should have known that permanence is not always a given.

My mother, Lydia, was the most beautiful and loving person I knew. This woman was born to be a mother, and she loved every second of it. Whenever I needed my mother, she was always there. She would pull me in for a hug, and the feeling of love and safety would radiate through my body. But on 23 June 2009 that all rapidly changed. My dad got a phone call saying we needed to go to the hospital straight away. I was 11 years old, just leaving primary school, heading towards a new chapter in my life. When we arrived, I knew it was bad news, that sinking feeling you get in the pit of your stomach. At the funeral I have never seen a church so full. We had family come over from Ireland on my dad's side, and my mother's family, who were from a Romani community. Some of the people at the funeral I had never met. They expressed how much they would miss my mother, while I was left confused about how they could ever miss her. I remember how so many people picked me up and promised they would always be there for me. However, when I was 13, staring at my entire life's belongings in a bin bag, I was left wondering where these people were and how could they break such a promise. As a matter of fact, when my mother died the family died along with it. Slowly, but surely, others started to disappear from my life. That feeling of unity, support and love was becoming a distant memory by the time I was 13.

I was brought into care on 10 October. I remember being picked up by a police officer and placed in a residential home. At this point my father could not be a father, and my sister didn't know where she fitted in. I had no biological family close to me; most still do not know

I went into care at all. I remember thinking of what my family would have thought if we lived in the 19th century. Romani and Irish values circulated in my head, and keeping your family together always stood out. Social services told me time and time again that keeping family together is of paramount importance. However, with my mother dead, my father not being around and no other biological family, my social worker was placed in a tricky situation. Before I knew it I was placed under a Section 20 Care Order. I did not understand what this really meant for me. I just knew life had changed forever. The people I always thought would be there for me in difficult times were gone.

Residential care was my new home; I remember the kindness of a boy in the placement who lent me his clothes while I had none with me. I was quickly moved again, to be given my 'forever foster home'. This family was meant to 'act' like my family. I found all this very strange, like I had been given the worst leading role. I was in a room full of strangers again, forced to accept my circumstances, with no control over my life. I caught myself staring at the other girls in the placement, terrified but weirdly defensive. These people had different life experiences, but we all had one thing in common: we could not live with our parents. The dread of having to tell my friends I was in care filled every gap in my body. When people talked about children in care, they spun negative statistics at me. I desperately did not want the statistics to become truth. I remember the social worker talking for what felt like hours about my role in this 'new family' and who everybody was. The new house smells, the dog, the posh ornaments dotted around and the pictures of strangers on the wall. I just wanted the world to swallow me up.

I remember curling up to sleep that night, terrified. I felt a poking at my leg and I shut my eyes tighter, willing to accept the darkness of the night to swallow me up. The poking did not stop. Frustrated, I opened my eyes to find a very teary young girl at bottom of my bed crying, telling me how she misses her family. Something very maternal kicked in. I opened my arms and cradled her to sleep. This young girl would often climb out of our bedroom window in the night to be with her family. While she was at a crossroads with adapting to life in care, she knew her family always loved her. I did not have that privilege of the feeling of love and warmth. The closest to that were my friends. I always ran off to be with my friends. That's the thing about being in care: you have so much red tape around to protect you it stops you having a normal life. The red tape alienates you; you are isolated and end up feeling like a jigsaw puzzle that someone got too bored to complete. I felt I belonged nowhere – although I did feel like my friends wanted me around. So, I did everything I could do to be with them. I was determined to have a normal teenage life. This led to the consequences of many missing person reports, many emergency meetings and a lot of telling off by strangers. I did not care about the consequences. I just wanted that feeling of belonging, and I got that with my friends. In a year of living in my placement I generally started to love my foster sisters like family. However before long one person would move out, followed slowly by the rest. Nobody stayed in touch. I still miss them now. I remember thinking I was never going to have a family like everyone else. I was quickly moved on after two years of arguments, meetings and paperwork. My foster carer cried when I left. I thought this was ironic as she was the one who gave me up. I thought, you have several biological children and you never once rang the police on them when they were late home from a party. You would never give your child up to a stranger, especially as you have never seen their home. You ring your child 20 times a day when they go on holiday, but you haven't rung me once since I left. But they were happy to give me up. I put my things in bin bags and moved on to the next place, an unregulated supported lodgement.

I hated being in care. I felt like I was a burden, an item that nobody knew what to do with. I looked around and saw the people who cared for me, but felt they only cared for me because they got paid. I wondered how this could be defined as a family when we do not class babysitters, teachers or social workers as family. Nothing made sense. Everyone around me used sterile words and described my situation to me like I was not the one living it. Sometimes I felt I wasn't. The only time I found peace was when I went to college. I surrounded myself with people I loved, and I felt safe. I dreaded going home when college finished, so would often wait around and come in on my days off. College was the first time I started to enjoy education. I met people who did not care whether I was from a council estate, in care or if I liked metal music a bit too much. Everyone accepted me for who I was. I felt I was part of a community. I was loved and wanted equally. My home life at the time was tricky. I was treated like family, although, when I looked around, I still didn't see my photos on the wall. I saw a difference in my relationships with their own biological children to me. Nevertheless, I felt loved. At the time, I was a young woman, going through normal teenage dilemmas. I was questioning my sexuality for the first time, learning about feminism and questioning my political views. Surprisingly, feminism and politics became my passions; although, on top of this, I was facing predicaments most teenagers do not have to face: questions of stability of placements. I was paying rent and bills and working 12-hour shifts; it was a huge weight of responsibility. I would go into college and act like everything was normal. I was living a double life, one being a mature adult and the other desperately trying to be a normal teenager. This was the first time I met another care experienced person outside where I lived. I felt an instant bond, like we just got each other and had each other's backs. I felt a shared sense of belonging and identity with them. It was the first time I questioned my care experience, as a positive sense of community, a joined belonging with others who have been in care.

My placement soon broke down, one month after I had spinal fusion surgery and months before I was due to start university. I decided to take Psychology at university. I felt optimistic. My friends, who now have become my family, were supporting me, and it was a brand new start. Going to university as a care experienced young woman was an eye-opening experience. I witnessed all the other students going for meals with their parents to settle in while I sat in my halls alone. My university friends often FaceTimed their parents to celebrate their success, while my friends rang me up to celebrate mine. Their parents took them to buy their university items. They could buy whatever they needed, while I was taken to Poundstretcher, on a strict budget, with my personal advisor and had to keep the receipts. I felt a disconnect from the other students around me. However, this feeling of disconnect was a feeling of normality for me now. I knew I was different to others, and the systems around me often liked to remind me of this fact. However, in all honesty, I was truly happy for the first time. My friends were now defined as my family, the university teams offering support and guidance and a feeling of pure stability and optimism. It was all finally looking up. Throughout my university career, my friends pulled me through the dark times and lifted me in times of celebration. I would not be here without them today – although they could not buffer the feeling of being the only care experienced person in the room.

In the later years of my undergraduate degree, my supervisor at the time opened me up to the idea that I could help other care experienced people. I was fascinated by this idea but did not see a future where this was possible. Before I knew it though, I was connected to the world of care experienced people through social media, thanks to a wonderful ally. This was a life-changing moment. I finally saw others who looked like me, had the same life experiences as me; and, most importantly, I felt like I belonged with them. I was part of a community. We all had a shared sense of identity with our care experience. It was almost like we communicated in a secret language that nobody else understood. We all knew our boundaries, what to say and what not to say, without really talking about it. It was very refreshing. By the same token, I felt naive around my brothers' and sisters' struggles. I only knew of how my care experience affected me and, ignorantly, never thought of others. However, once I knew, I couldn't stop learning and reading more. I shortly became an activist for other care experienced people who did not have a voice. I channelled my activism in every aspect of my life: in my education, to my friends and to society itself. Now, I cannot imagine a world where I am not fighting for the rights of others. It is my community, my family, my shared sense of belonging, and I will do anything to protect those in it. I now feel empowered and strengthened by my care experience. I am so incredibly proud of my life and every barrier I have overcome. Now, I have the most incredible care experienced family that surrounds me. We lift each other, celebrate our wins and guide each other, just like any other family. I have taken ownership of what family, belonging and community mean to me. I have redefined the barriers of such words, and it feels so good.

Currently, I am a PhD student. I now fall into a category that nobody cares to calculate as the system does not expect us to land in such positions. I live in a beautiful house with my loving partner of six years. My walls are plastered with photos of my family. My friends still surround me as any family would. My beautiful care experienced family continues to grow around me. I have broken every statistic and stigma thrown at me. I will continue to do so and champion others to also reclaim their lives. I am so proud of young me. I'm still navigating life as a young woman, questioning life, politics and my sexuality. I carry with me my hopes, family and optimism, and I have never felt so complete. While I will face new barriers, such as the Covid-19 pandemic, I am grounded by the fact I have my special people around me. I still have a lot to learn about my community. I am left without support from my corporate parents, as many care experienced people are, but my friends fill that gap. Many others do not have this. As young care experienced people, we are faced with poverty, lack of experience and stigma. Our local authorities, our workers and society have failed us. Circumstances like the pandemic only shine a light on these disparities. As an activist, a member of my community and a feminist, all I can do is fight for a better future for my care experienced family. I can only hope others will join our fight.

Discussion Points

Shaunna talks about chasing belonging. In what ways can belonging be cultivated for young people who feel familylessness?

Which relationships does Shaunna mention where belonging
   cultivation takes place?
How does Shaunna experience this?

Notes

1 https://allianceofcareexperiencedpeopleinhighereducation.home.blog/.
2 https://www.dictionary.com/browse/relationship.

Conclusion

When I started to embark upon the journey of this book, the whole exercise was to share lost and unheard voices. I wanted to open up a discussion, to provide some thought-provoking information for foster carers, teachers and staff in social care working directly with young people; but, essentially, it has turned out to have been an act of cathartic release for me. Many things that I was deeply troubled by have since evaporated, and the power not just of writing but of sharing one's writing has been felt.

While I was working on this book back in 2012 much happened that was incredibly poignant, and the landscape changed a little. The public unveiling of the Jimmy Savile inquiry altered many things. NSPCC director of child protection advice and awareness Peter Watt said: "The sheer scale of Savile's abuse over six decades simply beggars belief. He is without doubt one of the most prolific sex offenders we have ever come across and every number represents a victim that will never get justice now he is dead." Known to have actively targeted children in care (among many other vulnerable children), he has, from the grave, placed in the media spotlight the vulnerability of children in care who have been abused by people in power.

The busy media climate of interest in vulnerable children was a frenzy that had a uniqueness about it. Those of us who have been in care, and many who have worked in care, have known for years about the targeted abuse of vulnerable children. But Savile shoved this in the public's face until there was nowhere to hide.

In 2015 the Independent Inquiry Child Sexual Abuse commenced, and remains ongoing as I write. Not only focusing on children in care, it has also published on abuse in schools, health care, religious institutions, custodial institutions, residential institutions and sports.[1]

This 'new' climate of knowledge around abuse and vulnerable children means that there is a very real window of opportunity for change. I am hopeful about this because we live in a very different world of communication and awareness than we ever have before, and this can only be a useful positive thing in relation to improving the protection of vulnerable children. Maybe, just maybe, children will start to be protected in the way that they should have been from the outset – particularly when most of those children arriving into the system do so on the back of already having been neglected or abused.

*

In my own silence about my own story, I had failed to understand that this too was a shared response to spending time in care. I found that I was often the first person to whom the enclosed stories had been told in their entirety. I have had this said to me over and over again, and it's an honourable and humbling position to be in. It's not necessarily that people haven't shared their story before, but it will have been in bite-size chunks with little bits offered to different people at different times. This is much the way that I have told my own story over the years: a manageable collection of painless short stories rather than a gripping, emotionally torturous novel.

I found connection in the stories shared. The references on identity, loss, aloneness and boundaries just rang through me like church bell practice early on a Sunday morning, and they were always spoken by people with whom I really only had 'being in care' as a shared experience. The differences in everyone's stories – and those of anyone who I have ever worked with in a professional capacity – are always so diverse; but the similarities ring out as though we are from the same family, in the strangest possible way.

So, in my own reflection, what first really struck me was that the silence I lived with during my twenties and thirties was also a shared experience. The power of re-invention of the self and the fact that very few opportunities ever came up to discuss that part of my life meant that these things were often not spoken of. Whereas people talk about their families all the time, people who have been in care don't tend to talk about being in care. The point of reference isn't there. This has meant that some of the people in the book have friends who are not aware of their background. Having said that, I do believe that this has changed and words like 'community' and 'belonging' shine through as people talk about meeting others with the same experience.

The other shocking similarity that needs to be highlighted (as if it wasn't being highlighted enough in the media) is that most of the people I have met who have been in care have at some time experienced abuse, sat next to abuse or comforted someone who has been abused during their time there. There are many things that adults who have been in care do not speak of; but to the trained/experienced eye, we know, we understand and we 'see' what a person describing their time in care has experienced/is aware of. There are many details that are eliminated in this storytelling process, and I'm sure you understand why. We fill our lives with children, jobs, friends; there are things that don't need to be said explicitly but unfortunately are implicit in the experiences of many people.

And, finally, one of the great bonuses for me and a few of the other people that I spoke with for this book has been recognising our sense of justice and inclusion. Living in children's homes is a little like being in Heathrow Airport; it's a little piece of the whole of the world – all cultures, religions, disabilities and abilities living together in one space. Being homeless was no different. I shared spaces with people from every region of the UK. I expected, embraced, valued and was comforted by difference, long before it was written down in some sort of Policy and Procedure. It was my 'normal'.

Jane explained this through saying: "I didn't see difference. I didn't feel the difference. We were all just in care." This backdrop of diversity can have the potential for qualities such as compassion, understanding, tolerance and acceptance – a very positive outcome for care experienced people.

So, in conclusion, the positives and negatives sit uneasily side by side, encouraging some personalities to thrive and flourish, others to spend a lifetime searching for answers, and others again struggling to be who they might have been had life not dealt them this particular hand of cards.

I therefore believe that young people who come into care have to have the Very Best Parenting, Parenting Extraordinaire if you like. There has to be a chance that those who will flounder without a sense of belonging, or are at risk of predators, or are unable to meet the demands of a constantly changing education system, learn to develop other tools and strategies to have the best chance of flourishing. Good Enough parenting for these children is not good enough.

The development and nurture of social and support networks that encourage long-lasting friendships and foster a sense of belonging also have to be integral in the Very Best Parenting approach. My dissertation for my degree all those years ago had been about the lack of support networks provided for young people in care and the effects of that on self-esteem. Constant house/school moves, poor self-image, shame regarding circumstances and a desire for reinvention are some of the reasons why young people can be and feel so isolated from other young people. Creating spaces where young people can develop friendships and have shared experiences is integral to the work that I do. Watching those connections form by running groups with other local young people is a wonderful thing.

The most astounding feature of the personality of the care experienced has to be awarded to resilience. It is a skill rather than a trait, carried by those who have had to deal with a lot more than most; and it is this that underpins their ability to keep on going, keep on getting up again and keep on striving.

My own personal experience is that I was lucky. I was very lucky. At around my late teens and very early twenties the doors that had been shut tight were forced open by an alcohol problem that I didn't want to have and my arrival in a life of sobriety a day at a time. This happened to coincide with me being funded to go to university. Every emotional, educational and personal door opened, and I was like a sponge. I wanted to learn everything I could about how to build up the mess that I felt I was and how to learn all that I could about my chosen subject.

I was studying Sociology at a university that I thought had made some terrible mistake by allowing me to attend, having never written a proper essay before. I had scraped through a couple of A Levels at a college in a part-drunken, part-sober stupor; and here I was, now doing a degree.

Looking back, I now realise that this was a window of opportunity, and one that I'm not sure stays continually open without daily work and acknowledgment of it. I asked a few of the contributors their thoughts on this. They said that there was a period in their lives when they had become 'open' to personal development learning; and some of them took it, like I did, without even knowing it. Others missed that window of opportunity and had to wait another 20 years for the window to open again.

There are some important messages in this book that I hope will provide some new thinking – swiftly followed by those that can taking action.

In any situation, the best thing you can do is the right thing; the next best thing you can do is the wrong thing; the worst thing you can do is nothing.

Theodore Roosevelt

I have heard it said many times that if we want something to change we must change it ourselves. In September 2021, Terry Galloway[2] dreamt of and executed the idea of creating a central website that had every single local authority in England[3] and their local offer, available for all to access.[4] It covers every aspect of transitioning to adulthood, can compare local authorities and, for me, is the largest public call to action for change that we have seen. What can be achieved together is phenomenal when doing nothing is simply not an option.

Notes

1 https://www.iicsa.org.uk/about-us/timeline.
2 Terry can be found on Twitter at https://twitter.com/TerryGalloway.
3 Department for Education (2018) Local offer guidance: guidance for local authorities, https://assets.publishing.service.gov.uk/government/uploads/system/uploads/attachment_data/file/683703/Local_offer_guidance_final.pdf.
4 https://www.careleaveroffer.co.uk/.

Mentors

I found them amongst
the parents of other people
my friends' mothers
watching them put their
feet up on sofas
being tucked in with kisses
cries of "I love you,
Good night, Sleep tight"

I felt the love lacking
searched for it in all the
wrong places, I paid for
the privilege of someone
to guide me, teach me the
things I didn't know,
a therapist to show me,
how to love

I became a support worker
for others, who found life
a struggle, when really
I needed my own, someone
to show me how life worked
through mistakes of my own:

men, my depression, always
alluding anxiety humming

I searched the self help
shelves, read cover to cover
how to be… a parent, a worker
a good human being
to recover, from having
no mother, understanding
I did nothing wrong
at 16 abandoned again,
I tried to find safety in lovers,

If just one person had told
me they loved me, showed me
they cared, helped fight the
system a different life
could have appeared
one with less struggle
a parent forever, a significant other

However, 50 years on I'm still
alive, a gift not given to some
of my foster sisters and brothers
I found my way back
my wisdom, my light
my inner guidance, glimpsed
moments of love
a hug and a smile I can
give this to others, to
find their own mentors,
living forever, inside of their souls

Chrissy Kelly

Index